Making Love,

PLAYING POWER

Men, Women,
& the Rewards of Intimate Justice

✦ ✧ ✦

BY
KEN DOLAN-DEL VECCH
LMFT, LCSW

Published by
Soft Skull Press
An Imprint of Counterpoint LLC
2117 Fourth St
Berkeley CA 94710

www.softskull.com
www.counterpointpress.com

Library of Congress Cataloging-in-Publication Data available from the Library of Congress

ISBN-13: 978-1-933368-68-9
ISBN-10: 1-933368-68-3

10 9 8 7 6 5 4 3 2 1

Cover design by Michael Fusco
Interior design by Maria E. Torres, Neuwirth & Associates, Inc.

Printed in the United States of America
Distributed by Publishers Group West

For Barbara and Joseph,
who taught fairness.

For Erik,
whose spirit gives every reason to hope.

For your generation,
may you know love more than domination
and truth more than fear.

Contents

✦ ✧ ✦

Introduction | vii

1 Principles of Love for the 21st Century | 1

2 The New Problem with No Name | 13

3 What Patriarchy Teaches Men | 29

4 Is My Partner Listening-Impaired? | 55

5 A Closer Look at Power | 69

6 Recognizing Abuse | 95

7 Beware Therapists and Other "Helpers" | 131

8 Transforming the Male Code | 153

9 Men Can Be Heroes! | 179

10 Creating Lasting Change | 191

11 Dialogue | 217

Notes | 227
Appendix: Power & Control Wheel | 231
Acknowledgements | 233

Introduction

✦ ✧ ✦

What if the measure of a man was his willingness to love? What a different world this would be, and what a difference we'd find within family and couple relationships.

Men *can* love. To some people, this may come as a surprise. They still believe that men can't handle the emotional heavy lifting that love sometimes requires, and that only women can shoulder the real work of couple relationships. This kind of thinking finds its roots in patriarchy, the worldwide system that puts men in charge and assigns women service work, including the day-to-day work of maintaining relationships. The good news is that a growing number of people, men and women alike, no longer accept this arrangement. Instead, they seek couple partnerships based upon love, mutual respect, and fairness. Building such partnerships presents major challenges, however, because the world has a way of pulling us back into the old patriarchal mold.

This book will help you resist that pull and create lasting positive changes in your couple relationship.

Patriarchy hurts everybody. Amazingly, most relationship-help books tiptoe around this fact. Not this book. I describe exactly what this beast called patriarchy looks like, how it wreaks havoc upon couple relationships, and how we keep it alive despite the fact that it does none of us any good. I offer "principles of love" that provide firm ground for partnership, discuss the important roles that different kinds of power play within relationships, and describe what fairness looks like. I show you how to make healthy changes within your daily life. Using the information, exercises, and "action steps" within this book, you and your partner can build a lasting relationship based upon mutual respect and fairness rather than the old rules of patriarchy.

Whether or not it's overtly stated, most relationship-help books focus on women. In keeping with patriarchal thinking, these books presume that women are and always will be far more willing than men to take responsibility for relationship matters. But I see this pattern shifting as my male therapy clients claim an increasing degree of responsibility within their important relationships. This book focuses on men in order to promote this hopeful trend. I spotlight men's beliefs, expectations, and choices that often contribute to relationship problems but go unacknowledged—much less challenged—and in doing so, I bring much needed balance to the way we understand the relationship equation. My recommendations for both men and women show how to transform these patterns.

What I have to say will be deeply validating for most women and challenging, in a positive manner, for most men. Therefore, if you are male and reading this book at the request of someone who means the world to you, I commend you. You are already performing an act of love. If you are reading from your own initiative, regardless of your gender, I commend you for your act of self-love.

This book will lead you to change, and committing to change

means braving fear and uncertainty. I commend you for your courage. While a journey of change never progresses without some discomfort, it becomes easier when you have a clear destination in mind and a map that guides you there. I provide you with these essentials.

THE PLACES WE'LL GO

I grew up in the same world as you, learned the same things about what it means to be a man, and have done all the things talked about in this book. I'm always working toward doing better, but I know that I'm still far from perfect. In short, I am no better than the next guy. So this book does not come from a place of infallible authority; instead, it describes what I've learned from many teachers, mentors, clients, and loved ones during the four decades of my journey as a family therapist, organizational consultant, student of human diversity, partner, parent, son, friend, boy, man, and human being.

Though the book focuses on couple relationships, it is important to recognize that relationships never take place in a vacuum. I discuss patterns within our society and the impact these make on our most important relationships. I also emphasize the importance of children, parents, in-laws, siblings, friends, and coworkers in the lives of couples.

21st-century couples come in many different forms: married couples, committed partners who live together but remain unmarried, committed partners who live separately, opposite-sex couples, and same-sex couples. The principles and suggestions I offer apply to them all.

Because nothing sheds light on a subject better than real-life examples, I include many of them. They come from my family therapy and organizational consulting practice, as well as from personal life experiences. Additional examples come from stories shared by friends and colleagues. You will notice that I often mention the ethnicity, skin color, sexual orientation, age, and other characteristics of many of the individuals in these examples. I do this because I want to help you notice the discrepancies between stereotypes and the real world of human beings. Also, case examples help most when they include people with whom a wide variety of readers can easily identify.

Nine chapters conclude with a list of "action steps" for men, women, and couples. These will help you and your partner put new learning into practice immediately. Don't be surprised when the action steps instruct you to discuss what you're doing with close friends and ask for their monitoring and support. Our time-honored commitment to privacy, another one of those patriarchal rules, works against us when we seek healing changes within our relationships. Nothing helps us follow through on planned changes more than the support of loving friends. Prioritize the relationship changes you and partner seek over concerns about privacy and you'll be on the right track.

Because each chapter informs those that follow, I encourage you to read them in order. They are sequenced as follows:

- ✦ Chapter One addresses love: what it is, what it isn't, and how vitally important it is for each of us to shape an understanding of this term so we are prepared to make the most important decisions affecting our relationships.
- ✦ Chapters Two through Four explore the ways that men in our society are taught to understand themselves and behave within intimate relationships, along with the impact these patterns have on couples.
- ✦ Chapter Five illuminates the ways that power structures all relationships, including couple partnerships.

+ Chapter Six addresses the important topic of domestic and dating violence. I discuss abuse within this book about couple partnerships because the problem occurs with epidemic frequency and remains closely linked to other relationship patterns, much as we may wish it to be otherwise.

+ Chapter Seven emphasizes the importance of being an assertive and knowledgeable consumer when seeking counseling assistance. As you'll see, those who are supposed to offer help too frequently only add to the problem.

+ Chapters Eight through Ten promote lasting change. These chapters will help you build habits that sustain your most important relationships.

+ Chapter Eleven presents an imaginary dialogue between a reader and me. I answer questions that might be percolating in the minds of readers and are drawn from those that are frequently asked when I give talks on the subject of couple partnerships.

As you read on, please be gentle with yourself and those closest to you. Keep in mind that this book is about *learned* patterns rather than aspects of us that are gifts of nature and beyond our power to influence. Doing so will help you experience the book not as a tool for casting blame or a source of guilt and defensiveness, but rather as a resource that builds understanding and launches welcome change.

Principles of Love for the 21st Century

✦ ✧ ✦

"The principles of love are always the same in any meaningful bond. To love well is the task in all meaningful relationships, not just romantic bonds."

—bell hooks

Three weeks after we started dating back in 1980," Angela said, "Nick got all choked up one night while he was saying goodbye to me and said, 'Angela, I . . . I . . . I think I *"L"* you!' Well, I had no idea what he meant so I said, 'What?' Nick stared at me for a second before saying, 'You know, I feel *"the L word"* for you!'"

Angela and Nick, friends of mine who recently celebrated their twentieth wedding anniversary, laughed. We were enjoying dinner at one of our favorite Italian restaurants.

"I still have trouble saying *"the L word"* sometimes," Nick confessed. "I think it makes me feel vulnerable or something like that."

"That's right, you still do have some trouble saying it," Angela said. "But that doesn't bother me so much anymore because you show me in so many ways that make me feel loved—and that's what really counts!"

Nick is not alone in his discomfort with the word *love*. Many people, the majority of them men, shy away from it. Some men fear that admitting to love compromises their manhood. Some men and women, on the other hand, use *"the L word"* so loosely that it becomes a meaningless cliché. And then, there are those who believe love is an unknowable mystery, beyond the reach of language and rational discussion. These three perspectives result in lost opportunities for closeness and great confusion about a vitally important aspect of relationships. They also contribute to rampant irresponsibility, for if we believe that love is an unknowable mystery, then how can anyone be held responsible when they undermine it?

I want to help you move beyond this nonsense. If we are serious about improving couple partnerships, we have to find the courage to get very close to this word and explore its meaning. After all, don't most of us want to build our intimate partnerships on a foundation of love?

We deserve to grasp what love is and what it is not because holding onto a clear meaning helps us navigate the uneven and frequently mystifying terrain of intimate relationships. Our understanding of love, like the North Star, provides an invaluable reference point for setting and checking the course we chart within our most important relationships. The following seven principles, which together form a working definition of love, help shape that understanding. They come from my work with couples, families, and organizations, and are also influenced by the writing of notable cultural critics, including bell hooks and Barbara Kingsolver. As you read them, evaluate my ideas and the values they represent rather than accepting them passively. Thinking critically about what I have to say will help you clarify your own definition of love. Developing a definition that *you* are comfortable with will serve you well not only as you read this book, but, more importantly, as you move forward through life.

PRINCIPLES OF LOVE FOR THE 21ST CENTURY

+ Love requires action.
+ Empathy is essential to love.
+ Self-love thrives when we nurture loving connections with others.
+ Love needs constancy.
+ It takes time for love to heal.
+ Mature love values accountability.
+ Love prescribes equality.

LOVE REQUIRES ACTION

While love describes both feeling and action, it becomes important when discussing relationships to emphasize love as something we *do* rather than something we *feel*. Our actions make our mark upon the world, affecting everybody with whom we interact. I do not suggest that feelings are insignificant. Exploring the contents of our hearts and finding the words that identify what we discover there provides the starting place for knowing ourselves and sharing ourselves with others. However, love makes itself known primarily through what we do and how that doing affects others. We may feel love, fondness, affection, closeness, and desire within our own hearts, but the actions we take provide the clearest measure of our love. When we nurture, respect, support, encourage, and show affection to others, we *demonstrate* love through these actions. The feelings of love that reside within us provide a beginning, but they remain unknown to others until transformed into loving action.

Loving action takes many forms. Doing the laundry, washing dishes, shopping for groceries, vacuuming, dusting, caring for pets, changing the bed linens, cleaning out the refrigerator, and other routine household tasks demonstrate love when couples share a residence. Childcare and eldercare not only demonstrate love for the recipients, but also for your partner who shares responsibility for these loved ones. Most women know this. Men, many of whom have traditionally attended to yard work, auto maintenance, and other periodic tasks, are catching on to the loving importance of the more regularly needed contributions listed above.

EMPATHY IS ESSENTIAL TO LOVE

Empathy involves listening well, being observant, and imagining what it's like to be in our partner's shoes, on the receiving end of our actions. Empathy requires paying attention to our partner's feelings, thoughts, needs, and desires, and assigning them great value. Note the difference between intentions (what we'd like to see happen as a result of our actions) and the actual impact of our actions (the effects our actions have on another person). Recognizing the impact of our actions requires focusing on our partner instead of ourselves.

Remember, the love we bring to a relationship shows in the actions we take rather than in the feelings that are inside of us. Nobody has a window into another person's heart. Reminding ourselves of this fact keeps us focused on the effect our actions have upon others. When the recipient of our actions lets us know that they feel deeply acknowledged, valued, respected, and uniquely cared for, we know that we have been successful in loving.

Empathy sometimes instructs us to act in ways that run directly counter to our own feelings and intentions. For example, we may desire a relationship to continue but the other person wants the relationship to end. In such circumstances, we are wise to prioritize empathy over our own desires. It is an act of love to refrain from pursuing another person. Allowing the other person to move on with their life without a connection to us, despite our strong desire to remain close, demonstrates love.

SELF-LOVE THRIVES WHEN WE NURTURE LOVING CONNECTIONS WITH OTHERS

Self-love provides the foundation for our integrity, our experience of wholeness and belonging. Self-love empowers us to offer love to others. We love ourselves by taking care of our own needs so we feel protected, cared for, and valued. We demonstrate self-love when we make decisions that help us survive and thrive, including the decision to seek assistance from others whose support or expertise we need. Self-love empowers us to be a friend and parent to ourselves. We love ourselves when we are able to answer "yes" to the question, "Do I consistently treat myself in the way I would treat another person whom I hold in highest regard?"

Most men have learned to put their own needs first. Women in contrast generally learn to put the needs of others first. Consequently, self-love often presents more of a challenge for women than for men. Men, on the other hand, often need to learn how to balance self-love with love for others.

Self-love, like all love, reveals itself through action. I listened recently to a seventy-five-year-old lawyer say, "If you come to my office you will always see a vase of roses on my desk. I buy them fresh every few days because I love beautiful flowers. Also, anybody who knows me well knows that Thursday is my Indian food night. I spend the afternoon preparing a dish from my favorite Asian cookbook and treat myself to a quiet evening at home. For thirty years I was an alcoholic and never took care of myself. I was well into recovery when I started doing these things. When I first stopped drinking I couldn't believe how much love I got from the people in AA. Eventually that love began to seep in. I started believing that I was worth something. I started giving back to the community. Now I set up one meeting each week— you know, make the coffee and arrange the chairs—and I speak in AA meetings at least once a month. One day it hit me that it would be a good idea to start sending some love my way. I realized that God wanted me to love myself just like I'd learned to love the AA fellowship. What a revelation! I started doing these things like the flowers and my quiet evening alone when I cook for myself. Now they mean the world to me. Giving to myself is one of the ways I celebrate the love I share with my community."

Notice the time and energy this woman invests. Her acts of self-love move well beyond passing thoughts of self-affirmation or briefly spoken words of encouragement. She puts time and energy into doing loving things for herself.

Self-love sometimes requires making very difficult choices. When an intimate partner threatens, demeans, or disrespects us, leaving the relationship, despite our ambivalence, may be a necessary act of self-love.

Self-love differs from selfishness and pathological narcissism, which are isolating and self-destructive. When we love ourselves, we celebrate the value of other people and the importance of our relationships with them. We recognize that part of taking care of ourselves calls for maintaining loving connections with others. Self-love exemplifies the circular nature of all love. Our giving to others, gratifying in and of itself, also inspires those who receive our love to reciprocate. We nurture ourselves whenever we nurture others.

LOVE NEEDS CONSTANCY

Love needs *continuous, reliable* demonstrations of respect, honesty, kindness, fairness, trust, and responsibility. We can *only* sustain love through these actions. Many people who claim to love their partners regularly ignore, demean, or seek to control them. They follow these hostile actions with an apology and a story about "having a bad day" or a "momentary lapse in judgment." Everybody has exceptionally stressful days, but if we treat a loved one badly, it's our responsibility to make sure it doesn't happen repeatedly. *Too often, however, such behavior becomes a pattern.* While this pattern can be profoundly confusing because the hostility alternates with more positive behavior, eventually it becomes clear to most people that they are receiving something other than love.

IT TAKES TIME FOR LOVE TO HEAL

When love between intimate partners is damaged and they decide to stay together, healing takes time. Grieving the damage done requires time. It also takes time for a new history of constancy to unfold and trust to be restored. Patience, therefore, is essential to healing. Attempts by one partner to force the pace of healing and reconciliation will always be experienced by the other as additional damage. Couple relationships never heal through impatient demands or pleas, as these never inspire the recipient to feel loved. Instead of love, these actions are experienced as pressure and disrespect.

MATURE LOVE VALUES ACCOUNTABILITY

New love can blind. Mature love values honesty and accountability. This applies to all relationships, not just intimate partnerships. Our best friends do not blindly support our decisions. Instead, they respectfully provide us with honest feedback, letting us know when they feel our actions are likely to cause unpleasant consequences for others or ourselves. Making us accountable in this manner is more risky than offering unquestioning support as it means facing the potential for conflict or rejection. It takes courage to offer honesty and accountability to those we love. When we experience mature love for another person we may hold unconditional feelings of regard for them, but we do not unconditionally support their actions. We risk telling the truth, offering guidance, and allowing them to face the consequences of their decisions.

LOVE PRESCRIBES EQUALITY

We demonstrate a fundamental aspect of love by treating other people as our equals. *There is an essential connection between love and respect.* Sometimes a person we love can't handle all of life's challenges—children, people with certain disabilities, older adults who need support and assistance—but love requires that we value their humanity equally. We demonstrate love in such cases by taking responsibility for their safety, care, or guidance. While caring for children and the infirm, we watch carefully for their growing capacity for self-determination, and as it emerges we affirm and celebrate it. *There is an essential connection between love and nurturing.*

It was predictable that the institution of marriage would become less stable as it shifted historically from an economic arrangement between two individuals and their extended families toward becoming a loving partnership between equals. The traditional structure of marriage, tightly bound to patriarchy, prescribes domination of women by men, which is incompatible with love. Love promotes interdependence rather than domination.

Treating others as our equals requires that we challenge power differences, including those linked to gender. When one partner expects the other to nurture selflessly and endlessly—the other partner never getting a turn at having their personal aspirations become the couple's priority—this arrangement works against love. Love supports each partner's growth toward his or her fullest potential. Without fairness, love will not endure.

Most people want love to be the centerpiece of their intimate partnership, but mainstream American culture rarely addresses the topic with directness and clarity. The principles of love in this chapter provide you with a starting point. At the beginning of the chapter, I challenged you to evaluate the principles of love I present so that you arrive at *your own* definition. I repeat that challenge here. Continuously refine your definition of love. It will serve as a reference point for evaluating, enriching, and enjoying the lifelong course you chart through your most important relationships.

✦ ✧ ✦　**ACTION STEPS**　✦ ✧ ✦
MEN

1. List at least five activities that demonstrate love to your partner. Be specific. For example:

   ✧ Do my partner's laundry, making sure to keep like colors together so the clothes are not damaged; fold and put the clean clothes away when dry.

   ✧ Without being asked, pick up items at the grocery store that I know my partner likes—a favorite herbal tea or facial soap or fragrant candle, etc.

   ✧ Clean the microwave oven.

   ✧ Groom my partner's dog.

   ✧ Iron my partner's work clothes.

◇ Offer a foot massage.

◇ Call my partner's parents or siblings to see how they're doing and fill them in on recent developments in our lives.

◇ Take the lead in planning an activity, such as dinner out, or a weekend trip with my partner and two of their most valued friends or family members.

2. Write another list of loving actions directed toward people other than your partner. Examples include:

◇ Call my brother or sister to find out how their job search is going.

◇ Call my parents at least once a week to see how they're doing and fill them in on recent developments in my life.

◇ Write a card or send an email to a friend telling them why I value their friendship.

◇ Bring a cup of coffee to the security guard at my workplace's gate or front desk.

3. Make a commitment to follow through with at least one item on your first list every day and one item on your second list every week.

4. Talk your lists over with a male friend whom you trust and respect. Let your friend know that you're working on bringing more love into your life and that you'd like him to help you out by asking how you're doing with following through with the items you've listed.

5. Privately refer to your list at a specified time every day: at breakfast, during an afternoon break, or just before going to bed, for example. At these check-ins, do the following:

⋄ Add one or more new items (so your lists of loving actions steadily grow).

⋄ Take a moment to relish the impact that one of your loving actions had on another person during the last 24 hours. Remember their reaction and the way it made you feel.

✦ ✧ ✦ **ACTION STEPS** ✦ ✧ ✦
WOMEN

1. List at least five activities that demonstrate self-love. Be specific. For example:

   ⋄ Read for pleasure, or listen to music for one half hour without interruption.

   ⋄ Go to lunch with a friend.

   ⋄ Put $100 into my savings account.

   ⋄ Spend a weekend away with close friends.

   ⋄ Take ten minutes to close my eyes, relax my body, and breathe deeply.

2. Share your list with a friend whom you trust and respect. Let your friend know that you're working on bringing more love into your life. Ask him or her to help you out by asking how you're doing with following through with the items on your list.

3. Commit to following through with at least one of these activities daily.

4. Refer to your list at a specified time every day: at breakfast, during an afternoon break, or just before going to bed, for example. Review your list of activities, reflect upon those you did within the last 24 hours, and identify the benefits that you and your loved ones gained as a result.

✦ ◇ ✦ **ACTION STEPS** ✦ ◇ ✦
COUPLES

1. Compose *principles of love* that you both agree upon. Use the ones in this chapter as a starting point but feel free to revise them or create new ones all your own.

2. Discuss your principles of love with at least two friends who love and respect both of you.

3. Every day, make a point of noticing at least one action that your partner takes that demonstrates your principles of love. Thank your partner for doing it and be specific. For example, say, "When I came home and found that the sink was clean and the dog had been fed I felt like you really cared about our family—thanks for those acts of love."

2

The New Problem with No Name

◆ ◇ ◆

You may have heard the joke about the guy who loses his keys one night. He is stooped over and searching under a street lamp when a passer-by stops and asks, "Where exactly were you when you dropped your keys?"

"I was over there," the man replies, pointing to a poorly lit corner several yards from where he's searching.

"Then why are you looking over here?" asks the passer-by.

"Because the light is better here," the man answers.

That's exactly what happens when many of us search for the keys to what's going wrong within our intimate partnership. We look where the light is shining. And when it comes to relationship and mental health issues, for generations we have been shining the spotlight of scrutiny and expectation almost exclusively toward women, leaving what men have been doing unmentioned, unexamined, and unchallenged within that poorly lit corner. You see evidence of this in the endless parade of psychiatric diagnoses and other mental health labels for women who are "too emotional," "too unpredictable," "too cold," and even "too loving." Hysterical, histrionic, labile, borderline, frigid, and codependent are but a few examples. By comparison, I wish you luck in trying to find a psychiatric diagnosis for men who "flat line" when it comes to the range of feelings they express, or men who destroy their health and family relationships by spending eighteen hours daily at work, or men who sleep peacefully while neglecting to pay their monthly child support.

Our society's over-focus on females and corresponding under-focus on males when it comes to relationship responsibilities has allowed men's behavior to remain the immovable object around which everything else in relationships must revolve. The truth is, of course, that many of the keys to understanding and changing relationship difficulties can be found within patterns of male behavior.

As we begin to pay attention to what men are doing, however, it quickly becomes evident that there is not enough descriptive language available to succinctly capture what we're observing. This makes sense when you consider the newness of the task. We're confronting another aspect of the "problem with no name" that Betty Friedan tackled in her classic book, *The Feminine Mystique*. Nearly half a century later, patterns of male behavior that cause difficulties within relationships remain largely unexplored and unnamed.

We need to have a name for something in order to discuss it with any consistency of meaning. We need to have words for identifying a problem in order to work toward resolving it.

This chapter names a pattern typical of many men. I describe six examples in which men's choices cause difficulties in their couple and/or family relationships. You are likely to recognize yourself or your partner in these stories. As you read them, decide upon the words you would use to characterize *the problem*. Following the vignettes, I'll review my line of thought as I worked toward finding the best words to describe the men's behavior.

ANDREW AND GAIL

At its most benign, *the problem* can seem to be little more than the spark for a private joke shared by lovers. That's how it started between Andrew and Gail. At twenty-two years old, Andrew, a soon-to-be law student from one of Boston's first families, never seems to know what's going on when it comes to anything having to do with the couple's social plans. Ever since they announced their engagement four months ago, he's relied entirely upon his fiancée, Gail, to manage their busy social schedule. Before then, Andrew seemed to be a lot more on top of their plans. Gail, a twenty-four-year-old from a similar background who works as a paralegal, has begun to joke with Andrew about his "selective amnesia."

Even when *the problem* is little more than the spark for a private joke between lovers, however, its persistence is likely to ignite larger concerns. Gail increasingly finds herself irritated at Andrew's disregard for responsibilities that really belong to both of them. She wonders, "Does he think I'm supposed to be his personal secretary?"

CAROLYN AND GEORGE

With time, the ripening of relationships, and the addition of children, *the problem* often grows broader and deeper, as it has for George and Carolyn, an Irish-American couple who live in a working class suburban neighborhood. George rarely changes his nine-month-old son's diaper, but when he does the deed, he can be counted on to "forget" and leave the dirty diaper on the changing table, the baby's dresser, or the window sill, a gift for his wife, Carolyn, to discover, sometimes hours later.

George has other perplexing habits, like doing only his own

laundry because "I'm afraid I'll do something wrong and wreck someone else's clothes." This thirty-four-year old man, who manages a large group of people and operating systems for a living, seems to put aside many of his technical and administrative talents upon arriving home, as though passing through some unseen filter of consciousness at the front door.

Carolyn, also thirty-four years old and a corporate communications manager, spent one recent Saturday at home with the couple's three sons, aged sixteen, ten, and nine months. On this day, which found George at his job as a department store manager, Carolyn did the laundry (everybody's laundry), cleaned the house, made sure everyone was fed, got her middle son to his basketball game, and wallpapered a bathroom, all with her nine-month-old in tow.

On Monday, George's day off from work, he phoned Carolyn at her office at 1:00 PM asking her to come home. He needed to take a ride to his office in order to pick up his annual performance review paperwork so he could get an early start on it. Carolyn, realizing that the two older boys were at school and only Justin, the baby, was with George, asked him what the problem was. It turned out George felt he shouldn't have to "lug the baby" with him on this errand, having "put in enough baby time" that day. He went on to say that his recent schedule, which had him taking days off during the week instead of on the weekends, was "getting to be a real bummer" because, having the baby with him, he couldn't just unwind or hang out with his friends, like he could on a Saturday or Sunday. Carolyn, holding her tongue and counting one, two, three . . . slowly to herself, tried to remember the last Saturday or Sunday she spent relaxing with friends. When she felt calm enough to refrain from screaming obscenities at George, she launched into a familiar challenge regarding the relative amounts of time and effort they each put into taking care of the baby.

UMA AND JOHN

The problem, the pattern of male behavior that this chapter identifies and names, does not visit only white people, or people of a certain ethnicity, age, or social class. It often affects many areas within a relationship, while at first glance it may seem limited to a single point of disagreement. Uma, a Southeast-Asian-American obstetrician, and her husband of twenty years, John, a Russian-American research physician, argue about one thing—kayaking. John took up the sport eight years ago after he tried it out at a team-building weekend with his office mates. It did not take long for it to become John's obsession. So much so, in fact, that he has missed family weddings, their children's birthdays, and other important events because a kayaking trip or competition happened to be scheduled at the same time.

John lives for his twice-monthly kayaking trips during which he and a few of his male friends spend Saturday and Sunday training at a site fifty miles from home. John has recently begun to hate Uma's "nagging." The way he sees it, all her talk about jeopardizing his safety and taking too much time away from the family is a smoke screen—"She just doesn't respect my passion in life." John wonders what happened to the young woman who used to love everything about him. He has begun to question the future of the relationship.

STEVE AND MARY

The problem often shows up in the guise of helpfulness or protectiveness toward others. For instance, a man decides to "not bother" his partner with the details of a financial transaction involving the couple's shared assets. In the following example, the secret is more personal in nature.

Steve and Mary work for the same soft drink bottling plant that hired them twenty-four years ago, Steve as a maintenance technician and Mary as an office assistant. They had dated during their junior year in high school, and married at age twenty surrounded and embraced by their Portuguese-American families and Catholic community. Recently, the couple celebrated their twenty-second wedding anniversary at a surprise party thrown by their twenty-year-old twin sons, Evan and Peter.

While from the outside everything might appear to be going well for this couple and their family, Steve hides a secret. Two years after his marriage to Mary, shortly after the birth of their sons, his struggle to suppress his desire for other men turned a corner. He began acting on these feelings, engaging in anonymous sex at highway rest stops not far from his home. Steve discusses this with nobody, feels ashamed of the double life he leads, and grows increasingly depressed. He considers talking with Mary about it but always concludes that the better course is to stay quiet, telling himself that this will "protect her."

Mary senses that something is wrong, and she's been worried about Steve's preoccupation and moodiness for a very long time.

AARON AND CHARLES

The problem doesn't even require people of different sexes. It's perfectly willing to crash gay relationships too. Aaron and Charles, both thirty-seven years old, have lived together in New York City for six years. Both men are "out" as gay men to their families, coworkers, and friends.

Aaron is a self-proclaimed "Chelsea boy," which means he spends a lot of time working out at the gym and paying attention to his appearance in other ways as well. White, and of mostly Italian-American heritage, he works as a human resources manager at a large corporation where his colleagues like and respect him. Aaron prides himself on his good looks and ability to attract attention.

Charles, black, his family originating in Trinidad and moving to the United States shortly after his birth, makes his living as a waiter. Chubby, not particularly concerned about his personal appearance or that of others, he favors the world of culture and ideas. During the day, he studies painting and sculpting at a prestigious university fine arts program where a number of his professors believe he shows great potential. Charles works evenings at the restaurant, and frequently needs to stay on the job well into the early morning hours on Saturdays and Sundays.

Each member of this couple declares sincere feelings of love for his partner, stating to each other and to friends that he believes they complement one another beautifully. Both partners describe their strong commitment to the relationship. At Aaron's insistence, however, they have an open relationship, meaning that both are allowed sexual liaisons with other men. Their agreed-upon rules include consistent safer sex practices, excluding mutual friends as sexual contacts, refraining from using their home as a meeting place with other sex partners, and being completely open and honest with one another if questioned about these liaisons. Aaron enjoys this arrangement. Charles, on the other hand, feels saddened by his partner's desire for sex with other men but tolerates the agreement. He abstains from having sex with others and has no interest in asking Aaron to describe his extra-relational activities.

JUDI AND JAY

The problem can also create so much hostility and confusion that it begins to derail one or both partners' sanity. Jay, a twenty-six-year-old Anglo-American database analyst, can't understand why

Judi, his twenty-five-year-old German-American fiancée, is so moody. "We used to have so much fun together. Now she's gotten so serious that I'm beginning to wonder if she's depressed."

Three months ago, Jay and Judi moved in together. Two months later, Jay announced to Judi that a "minor issue" had arisen. Susan, an old girlfriend with whom he had had a tryst nine months previously during a brief separation from his relationship with Judi, was about to give birth to his child. Jay matter-of-factly stated that he had no feelings for Susan and did not want any involvement in the child's life, but would like to provide financial support. He planned to meet with Susan and a mediator because she wanted a written agreement. Jay also informed Judi that he did not want to talk about the matter. "I don't want to get preoccupied and have it affect my work performance. The way I see it, it's kind of a sore point for me; I made a bad choice and I'm doing what's necessary to resolve the issue." He also asked Judi not to discuss this with others as he considered it extremely private.

Upon hearing this news, Judi became distraught. She had no idea Jay had been involved with anybody during their month-long separation and felt furious about his silence on this matter, a matter in which she saw profound implications for their present relationship as well as their plan for a future together. Her feelings were all over the place. She experienced disbelief, outrage, betrayal, confusion, and despair—the whole spectrum of grief. Plus, there were a million questions Judi wanted Jay to answer.

Jay was talking the matter over daily with his father and brother, both of whom are attorneys. True to his initial proclamation, he didn't want to talk about it with Judi. All of Judi's questions were met with either irritation or dejected comments about how she didn't seem to care about how hard this was for him and his need to deal with it in his own way. Jay felt that Judi was becoming overbearing.

Judi found it immensely stressful to carry this burden all alone but persevered in keeping the story confidential. She found herself at times spending what seemed like hours wondering about this child, who she'd recently learned was a little girl—so many questions. One afternoon Judi asked Jay if he could honestly say that he never wanted to meet his child. He glared at her, telling her once again that this was none of her concern, that it was a very uncomfortable matter for him to talk about with her, and that he wanted her to trust him on this. Judi, having reached her limit, blasted him for failing to recognize that this was her concern as well as his.

"Do you have even the slightest idea of what it's like to deal with this all alone! You don't seem to think for one instant that this is something I'm dealing with, too! This involves a little girl, a real human being. It's not just about an agreement or a contract with Susan. And that little girl, because she's your daughter, is part of my life, too!"

Looking at her in disbelief, Jay said, "I CAN'T BELIEVE HOW SELFISH YOU'RE BEING!"

Later that evening, Jay, who had put their previous argument aside hours earlier, cheerfully asked Judi if she'd like to go out for dinner. He was dumbfounded when her response was to shake her head and burst into tears. He had no idea why she was crying, and began fearing that she might urgently need psychiatric attention.

The thread of male behavior that weaves through the relationships described above is uncomfortably recognizable and close to home for most of us men (and women). The words chosen to name that thread need to capture its essence as precisely as possible. In order to show you how I arrived at those words, I'll start by reviewing the themes these stories illustrate. Although the vignettes above don't represent every aspect of *the problem*, they exemplify the following:

+ Delegating to one's partner (usually by default) responsibilities for maintaining social connections.
+ Refusing to gain competence with housework and infant care.
+ Refusing to juggle childcare and other home life responsibilities with work-related responsibilities.
+ Unself-consciously prioritizing one's own feelings and desires over those of one's partner and other family members.
+ Claiming the right to make far-reaching decisions on behalf of other people without even consulting them.
+ Forgetting about one's partner's distress or other strong feelings even when they were expressed recently.

I considered a number of descriptive terms before arriving at the one that fit best. *Typical male behavior* came to mind first, but that term is not specific enough. It's also unfair because it indicts everything we men do without providing a clue regarding what needs changing. The word *sexism* is too broad. Sexism describes the ways in which the world is set up to oppress and discriminate against women and girls. It also describes the actions of institutions and individuals when they inflict injustice against females. *Male privilege* fits a little better because it refers directly to men, the people who most frequently enact the problem. As the flipside of sexism, however, this appellation is also too broad and perhaps a shade too impersonal. Male privilege describes all the ways that men and boys receive and claim special opportunities and status within our society. The word I sought needs to have a bit more personal agency. After all, it's one thing to be granted a privilege by the world, but we take it to another level when we repeatedly make choices that exercise that privilege, and do so at the expense of others whom we profess to care deeply about. I considered *selfishness,* but that word is too personal and malevolent in its meaning. Moreover, individual motives drive selfishness, and it's the collective experience of men and boys that drives the phenomenon we're trying to name.

The term that works is *male entitlement.* These two words best identify the self-serving attitudes and behavior that characterize the problem. Male entitlement is the pattern in which we men prioritize and enact our own thoughts, feelings, and desires without adequately consulting or even considering the implications for those closest to us, and, in most cases, without even noticing that we are behaving in this fashion. In other words, it is blind disregard for the inconsiderate nature of our pattern of choices.

Finding the words "male entitlement" to name attitudes and behaviors that cause relationship problems—but generally go unnoticed because they're widely accepted as the natural order of things—is a vital first step toward change. After all, you can't change something without first having words to describe exactly what needs changing. Another way to say this is that naming male entitlement expands our critical consciousness. *Critical consciousness is the state of awareness that results when we begin to examine relationship patterns that we had previously accepted without question.* As critical consciousness expands, windows onto new possibilities for change open.

Consider this example. Imagine that a man declines an invitation from his fiancée to take a day off and travel with her on a weekend trip to Bermuda. The trip was not planned, but rather a last minute opportunity that fell into his fiancée's lap. Going with her would put him slightly behind on a project at work. When asked why he declined, the man responds, "I have responsibilities, and I don't feel comfortable taking a day off without more notice." With a bit more critical consciousness, he would realize that he equates "I have responsibilities" with "I have responsibilities *to the workplace*." He would, further, realize that this rather narrow definition of his "responsibilities" (a definition shared more commonly by men than by women) prioritizes work over all other commitments. Recognizing that his definition of "responsibilities" *can* be broadened would free him to be less rigidly certain of where his or any person's first responsibility lies. He would question his belief that a man's first responsibility belongs to the workplace. He would at least consider that a man's first responsibilities may be to his own health and sanity, and perhaps to the relationship he's building with his life partner.

Considering these possibilities might also lead him to review the impulse that entitled him to make the decision all by himself, with no input from his fiancée. After all, this decision has an impact upon her. As the example illustrates, the development of critical consciousness complicates decision-making because choices are no longer preordained, but it also adds greatly to the potential quality of life and relationships.

Well, now that we've got *male entitlement* to name a pattern that causes many problems in couple partnerships, what next? Chapter Three looks into some of the ways that boys and men are taught to understand themselves and their role in the world, and there I'll explore with you some of the "training" that leads to male entitlement.

There is one last point I'd like to emphasize before moving on. The problem identified in this chapter is male entitlement, not people who happen to be men. There is a big difference. The first is a collection of learned patterns that shape the way one understands and interacts with the world and the second is a class of human beings, each of whom possesses free will and a wide range of behavioral options from which to choose. We men live in a world that since childhood has taught us to believe and behave in ways that are often destructive to our relationships. This is not a personal failing. Upon recognizing the fact that we live in such a world, however, we confront an array of confusing and very personal challenges. While I don't have all the answers, I know that a retreat into denial and defensiveness is not among them, nor is a collapse into immobilizing guilt likely to be productive. We can best move forward with courage and a spirit of open-minded inquiry, recognizing that male entitlement does not work very well for many people, including most men. It's time for us to work together toward making some long-overdue changes.

Here is the list, from page 30, that characterizes male entitlement. Refer to this list for each set of action steps that follows.

+ Delegating to one's partner (usually by default) responsibilities for maintaining social connections.
+ Refusing to gain competence with housework and childcare.
+ Refusing to juggle childcare and other home life responsibilities with work-related responsibilities.
+ Unselfconsciously prioritizing one's own feelings and desires over those of one's partner and other family members.
+ Claiming the right to make far-reaching decisions on behalf of other people without even consulting them.
+ Forgetting about one's partner's distress or other strong feelings even when they were expressed recently.

✦ ✧ ✦ **ACTION STEPS** ✦ ✧ ✦
MEN

1. Describe the unfairness that each of the examples of entitlement creates and what it would be like to be on the receiving end when a partner behaves in this manner.

2. For each item on the list above, write the pattern that would eliminate this aspect of entitlement. For example, for the first bullet you may write, "Share with my partner the responsibility for maintaining our connection to each other and to other people who are important to us."

3. For each of your new patterns, generate at least three specific opportunities that will put the pattern into action. Keeping with the same example, you might list:

   • When my partner and I agree that we'd like to get together with two close friends for an evening, at least half of the time I am the one who calls those friends to figure out the details of our get-together.
   • I make suggestions regarding activities that my partner and I might enjoy doing alone together. After we've decided on a plan, at least half of the time I am the one who gets tickets, makes reservations, and/or does any other necessary preparations.
   • When my partner and I decide to invite extended family members to our home for a visit, at least half of the time I am the one who contacts the family members and works out the details.

4. Review your patterns and the opportunities for each. Make a commitment to follow through on these action items, and keep a journal on your progress.

5. Discuss what you're doing with one or two male friends whom you trust and respect. Ask them to help you keep to your plan.

✦ ✧ ✦   **ACTION STEPS**   ✦ ✧ ✦
WOMEN

1. Identify specific instances when men who are important to you demonstrate each item of male entitlement, and write them underneath each respective bullet. For example, under the third bullet: "My partner always expects me to leave work and pick up our son whenever there is early dismissal at his grammar school, even though we both work and early dismissal days are scheduled months in advance."

2. Next to each example, write down steps you can take that will challenge the man to replace this aspect of male entitlement with fairness. Keeping with the same example, you might write: "I will tell my partner that we need to go over the school schedule together, and that I need him to split the responsibility of picking up our son from now on."

3. Make a commitment to follow through with the steps you've written down. Discuss your intentions with one or two friends whom you trust and respect. Make an agreement to check in with these friends on at least a monthly basis for support.

✦ ✧ ✦   **ACTION STEPS**   ✦ ✧ ✦
COUPLES

1. For each item, write a statement describing the pattern that eliminates this aspect of entitlement. For example, for the second bullet: "We share responsibility for housework and childcare in a manner that each of us considers fair."

2. Make a commitment to put your "Code of Fairness" into action immediately.

3. Schedule a "partnership meeting" once a week. At that meeting, give your partner specific feedback about times during the previous week when their actions exemplified your Code of Fairness. You don't have to wait for this weekly meeting, however. During the week, thank your partner whenever you see them doing something that exemplifies the code.

4. Invite two friends whom both you and your partner trust and respect out to dinner. Let them know what you're doing and ask them to support your efforts by letting you know when they see that you're living up to the code, and, even more importantly, perhaps, when they see that you could do better.

3

What Patriarchy
Teaches Men

✦ ✧ ✦

"A ct like a man!" shouted the red-faced community health
educator, pretending to be a disappointed and infuriated
father confronting his son. With his jaw clenched, he glared and
shook his finger in the face of the sixteen-year-old student volunteer who stood facing him. The two then froze to signal the end
of their role-play.

The young man's high school classmates, seated in a circle
surrounding the pair, looked on in silence. Despite every student's underlying realization that the exchange they had seen was
part of the school's day-long program of "citizenship training" and
nobody was really going to get smacked or humiliated, the ten-
sion from their personal associations to the role-play filled the
room. After allowing a moment for the young people to come
back from their solitary reflections, the trainer pressed forward
with the exercise, one of a series devised by renowned teen violence prevention experts Allan Creighton and Paul Kivel. He led
the teenagers into a lively discussion about the challenge to "act
like a man."

The group arrived at a number of rules that capture the essence of American manhood. From there, they moved on to list the people in a boy's life who teach him how to act like a man: parents, teachers, coaches, religious leaders, and friends. Finally, they discussed the abusive tactics these people use to regain compliance whenever a boy steps outside the rules: name-calling, threats of ostracism, and physical assault.

This chapter, like the classroom exercise I just described, examines the male code, the collection of rules and expectations that boys and men live by. Rarely seen in print and hardly ever mentioned directly, some readers may wonder whether the code really exists. Nevertheless, I challenge you to gather any group of people and ask them the question: "What are the rules that men in this society are expected to follow?" You'll find small variations across the responses of individuals, of course. That's because the template for male identity that each of us holds is influenced by experiences that are particular to people with our ethnicity, sexual orientation, social class, religious affiliations, regional customs, and family background. Individual temperament also plays a role. However, when you ask for a group's consensus on the "traditional" rules of American manhood, most of us can easily agree on the major themes. I'd be surprised if you didn't come up with a fairly solid consensus within and across each group you polled.

Boys start learning the male code very early in life. Countless interactions with adults teach it subtly but with impressive consistency. We learn the code through the toys that adults hand to us versus those they take away if we happen to pick them up from our sister's toy box, the activities adults encourage us to engage in versus those they steer us away from, and the interests of ours that adults affirm versus those they discourage. Expectations of how we ought to express ourselves also teach and reinforce the rules. Remember, "Big boys don't cry!" Before entering kindergarten, most boys are beginning to learn that following the rules of the male code is essential if you want to fit in. It's even more fundamental than that. Following the rules is necessary to avoid physical and emotional assault. Any first grader can tell you that it would be dangerous on many levels for a boy to bring his favorite doll to school for playtime during recess or aftercare.

The good news is that times have changed and today's man is unlikely to follow traditional male roles with anything close to the kind of dedication typical of previous generations. The century that recently drew to a close witnessed the escalation of social movements demanding equality for women, people of color, gay men, lesbians, and transgender people. The systems that limit equality for each of these groups are tightly interwoven— they are all connected to patriarchy. As movements for social justice challenged these systems of inequality, they also began to shake up the rules of manhood. One result was increased flexibility within the expectations placed upon boys and men. It is important, though, to take a close look at those rules from yesteryear, because they still influence individual choices and relationship patterns in significant ways. They provide the foundation upon which men's feelings of entitlement rest.

RULES OF THE MALE CODE

RULE 1: *Don't act like a girl!*

RULE 2: *Keep your feelings to yourself!*

RULE 3: *Work is your first priority!*

RULE 4: *Be self-reliant!*

RULE 5: *Be aggressive!*

RULE 6: *Be dominant!*

RULE 7: *Women are for sex!*

RULE 8: *Don't be gay!*

This list of rules is adapted from the work of family therapy researcher Robert Jay Green. While they are numbered for easy reference, the order of the rules is not meant to convey relative significance. You will also note that, far from being entirely discrete, the rules interconnect and sometimes overlap. Please be advised that I do not presume this list to be complete. Rather, it captures the patterns that are most helpful to our discussion of intimate relationships.

As you read through the expanded descriptions of the rules that follow, please keep in mind the following observation: none of us is ever entirely alone, operating as a completely free agent, within any of our relationships. Instead, each of us brings into every relationship strong connections to all of the identity groups, or communities, that contribute to our self-image. By the time each of us engages in adult-to-adult relationships we are already firmly grounded in a number of these communities: the community of men, the community of middle-class people, the community of white people, and our community of faith, for example. Our lifelong connections to these groups profoundly shape the attitudes, feelings, and behaviors we bring into each personal encounter. A challenge faces us, therefore, to recognize the impact of our community connections in terms of the privileges we take for granted and the prejudices in which we've been indoctrinated. Accepting this challenge marks the beginning of one's journey of critical consciousness, a journey whose rewards can be greatly increased awareness of the social forces driving interpersonal behavior, a more self-assured understanding of personal accountability, and a lifetime of more satisfying relationships.

1

R U L E

Don't Act Like A Girl!

In the locker room at New York Sports Club, I overheard two middle-aged men joking with one another after their exercise class. In their good-natured banter, the first man chided the second about how tired he seemed toward the end of the class.

"Ed, you seemed to have a heck of a time keeping up today— are you feeling okay or maybe just getting old?" "I don't know, man," Ed replied, "but what's up with those shoes you're wearing? I've noticed that all the girls wear them but no other guy besides you!"

Both men laughed.

Ed's statement was the adult man's variation of the "You throw like a girl!" epithet Little Leaguers dread. Even when delivered in jest, the underlying rule comes through loud and clear: real men do not behave like or resemble females in any way, shape, or form. Within Ed's statement, note his appellation "girls" for the women participating in the exercise class. The persistent habit some men have of calling women "girls" belies a biased perspective on the relative status of men and women. One can easily draw the analogy to when white slave owners referred to slaves as children: "boy," or "girl," regardless of their age.

The rule that maleness must be defined in opposition to and with higher status than femaleness has pervaded all aspects of family and community life. It has contributed to a fundamental imbalance in respect and power that continues to have far-reaching consequences. The results show that boys and men:

+ refuse to learn tasks traditionally assigned to women,
  such as laundry, housekeeping, and childcare.
+ lean toward certain interests, sports, artistic pursuits,
  hobbies, and occupations, and away from others.
+ find difficulty accepting the authority and leadership of women in a variety of life spheres, including
  family matters, politics, and the world of work.

RULE

Keep Your Feelings To Yourself!

Tom, a fifty-year-old man of Czech-American background, like
many his age, had uncertain prospects in the highly competitive
job market of the moment. He had learned during the previous
week that his job as an insurance claims adjuster was being elim-
inated as part of a large-scale downsizing. After working for his
company for the previous four years, and having worked for only
one other employer since leaving high school, Tom would receive
severance amounting to twelve weeks' salary.

The human resources consultant at Tom's place of work
referred his wife, Jessica, to me. Jessica was six years younger
than Tom and from an Italian-American family background. She
had no idea how the family was going to cope with the loss of
Tom's income and was distraught during our initial phone conversation. Apparently, the couple had not been able to put aside
much in the way of savings and with children aged fourteen, seventeen, and nineteen—one in college and two on the way—Jessica said she had no idea what to do. What concerned her even
more, she said, was the manner in which Tom was behaving.

"It's like nothing at all has happened! No tears, no sadness, no anger even!" she said. "I can't figure this out. I feel like Rome is burning and all he's missing is his fiddle! I wonder if there's something wrong with me, or with him! I feel like I'm going crazy!"

We scheduled a time for the couple to come to my office the following day. After they arrived, I met with the pair together to get a sense of their joint description of the problem. Jessica did most of the talking, despite my efforts to engage Tom. I then asked to meet separately with each of them, Tom first. He told me that he was terrified about what would happen next but saw no point in "getting hysterical about it like Jessica." Although he chose the word *terrified,* Tom's expression remained flat. Like many men, he seemed hobbled when it came to his range of emotional expressiveness. I asked him if he had told Jessica how scared he was feeling. He said, "No, I don't want to upset her any more than she already is." He also told me that he was working on a few employment leads already and "would just keep at it until something clicked." He hadn't shared his determination and hopefulness with Jessica either, saying he feared that she'd worry if he got into the subject of his job search at all with her. I advised him that sharing his fears and uncertainties with Jessica, contrary to what he imagined, would be unlikely to add to her level of distress.

"If you tell Jessica that you're frightened, this will mark her own fear as reasonable and appropriate," I explained, "and knowing that you and she feel similarly about what's going on will help her feel more calm and closer to you."

A short while later when I had the couple back in the same room with me, I encouraged Tom to share with Jessica what he'd described for me. Hesitating at first, Tom pushed forward. He said, "Jess, I've been really frightened about the possibilities but I didn't want to add to your burden. I also didn't want to get bogged down in fear. I'm working really hard on finding and following up on some leads and I figured that was the best place to put my energy."

Jessica relaxed considerably. She said, "I'm so glad to hear you talk this way. I feel so much less alone knowing this is hard for you, too. I mean, I figured it had to be had to be hard for you, but you were like a stone. Now I can begin to feel like we're in this together."

Tom was following Rule #2 partly as a misguided effort to spare his partner emotional pain. In doing so, he presumed that he alone should make the decision to shield her from his feelings without even asking her first whether this would be her choice. Evidently, Tom, like many men, had been adhering to this rule for so long that he only reluctantly shared his feelings, *even with himself.*

When boys and men have been living all their lives by axioms like "Big boys don't cry" that equate openness and vulnerability with personal weakness, this kind of unfamiliarity with one's own feelings often develops. Often, those boys and men who are taught to equate expression of most feelings with weakness in fact do acknowledge and express one feeling more strongly than all others. That feeling is anger. Anger is allowed to surface because its expression is perceived as powerful, and experience shows that displays of anger often gain compliance from others. In fact, many men have learned to collapse a whole range of feelings—fear, sadness, disappointment, frustration, uncertainty, self-consciousness, embarrassment, and confusion—into anger. Their inclination toward anger, coupled with little experience and interest in identifying and expressing most other feelings, creates great difficulty within intimate relationships.

Finally, Rule #2 has important implications for male physical health and well-being. Many men are so distant from their feelings that they disconnect from their bodies, allowing themselves to accumulate numerous symptoms of health problems without responding appropriately. I'm talking about things like obesity, shortness of breath, fatigue, and various recurrent aches and pains. Ignoring one's health has the potential to seriously limit or interrupt all aspects of one's life. At the very least, when men who are engaged in intimate relationships do not take adequate care of themselves, this places a burden on their intimate partners, who often feel compelled to take a parental attitude. Viewed in this light, each person needs to make self-care a primary task in order to demonstrate responsibility and respect toward themselves and their partner.

RULE

Work Is Your First Priority!

A friend of mine recently told me about a conversation he had with his brother, Mark, who lived and worked in New Haven, Connecticut, and had just decided to accept a job offer in Los Angeles, California. Mark, a recently divorced thirty-five-year-old Italian-American man, enjoyed success as an attorney. Jolie, his ex-wife, had physical custody of the couple's two daughters, aged nine and seven. My friend told me that Mark saw no conflict at all in moving several thousand miles away from his daughters' home, saying that he'd negotiated with his new employers the freedom to fly back to Connecticut for a long weekend once every month. My friend described how he tried to convince Mark that one long weekend a month was not enough for either Mark or his daughters. My friend shook his head and said, "When I was done with my pitch, Mark looked at me like I was crazy and said, 'This job is the opportunity of a lifetime. I'm sure my kids will understand!'"

Another situation reveals a similar pattern. A new client named Jack came to see me for a consultation because he was exhausted and worried. Forty-three years old, African-American, he was working as a director for a technical support team at a major corporation. Jack and his wife, Dana, also African-American, were the proud parents of Rudy, their nine-month-old son.

"I have worked thirty days straight, right through Presidents' Day Weekend, and I'm averaging seventeen hours a day here at the firm. I can hardly sleep and my stomach is giving me such problems that I've only been able to eat Jell-O most days for lunch if I want to keep anything down. Actually, Jell-O is about all I've had time for. My gastroenterologist told me six weeks ago that I'm doing serious damage to my stomach and esophagus—I guess all my stress goes right to my gut."

When I asked him to consider putting his health first by setting limits on the hours he works every day and refusing to work weekends, he responded, "The project is going really well and I want to keep it that way. I'm proud of my work and the work the rest of the team is doing. This pace should calm down in five weeks. Can't you give me some ideas on how to lessen the stress I'm feeling?"

I told him there were no magic words and that only taking care of the basics, including rest, good nutrition, emotional support, and exercise, would help him regain balance.

"But I've got a job to do!" he explained.

I pushed him a little further by asking, "What's more important, your health and sanity, along with time spent with loved ones, or getting this project done?"

He didn't even have to think for moment before responding: "Right now, this project is top priority. I might end up in a hospital before it's over, but getting the job done means that much to me."

As I mentioned at the start of this chapter, we bring many community connections into our everyday interactions. As an

African-American man, Jack's choices are likely influenced not only by the male code, but also by ongoing racial oppression within our society. In *From Brotherhood to Manhood: How Black Men Rescue Their Relationships and Dreams from the Invisibility Syndrome,* Anderson J. Franklin writes of black men: "Many of us have learned . . . that to get ahead you have to work 'day and night.' That message is also coupled with implicit and explicit messages that we should be prepared, as African-American men, to work twice as hard and be twice as good."

The willingness to suffer physical and emotional damage in order to satisfy the demands of employment is not exclusive to any racial or ethnic group, however. In a more humanistic world, there would likely be a diagnostic term for this kind of inverted prioritization. *Workaholism* comes close, but our society has co-opted this word in a way that makes it seems almost virtuous nowadays. Sometimes originating within individuals, sometimes driven by the demands of a workplace's management, and most often derived from a fair measure of both, the ruthless expectation that work will take priority over all other aspects of men's lives continues to be a major theme in our society, despite all the lip service many corporations now give *work/life balance.*

Rule #3 contributes to many types of difficulties within family and couple relationships, in addition to the painful distancing of parents from their children and from each other. Men too often believe that since their main commitment belongs to the world of paid employment, they bear little or no responsibility for "second shift" duties. In other words, many men feel that since they "work all day," this entitles them to refrain from doing the unpaid work of maintaining a home and family connections. The second shift includes all the things people do in order to keep their lives intact: monitoring inventory of food and other household supplies, making lists of items that have to be purchased, shopping for groceries and other necessities, meal preparation, housework, and doing the laundry. The second shift also includes childcare, supervision of homework, managing social connections for the family, and managing other family/community administrative responsibilities like the scheduling of medical and dental appointments, play dates, birthday parties, scout meetings, and parent/teacher conferences.

When men feel entitled to exempt themselves from second shift responsibilities, it puts enormous pressure on their partners and other family members.

Neglect of second shift tasks also results in many lost opportunities for men. While often very hard work, these tasks center upon nurturing and caregiving, both of which are instrumental in building human bonds. Bathing, dressing, and feeding our little ones, comforting them when they're not feeling well, tucking them in and reading bedtime stories, sharing mealtimes together as a family—these make priceless experiences for parents and children alike. It's a loss for all involved when men decide not to participate.

I recently learned that a forty-three-year-old white corporate executive, upon learning that he had inoperable pancreatic cancer, undertook extraordinary measures at his office and within his work group to ensure that he would be able to spend the remaining few months of his life largely at the workplace. He told colleagues who urged him to take more time for himself and his family that the company needed him and he felt most comfortable in the office. One can only imagine the impact this decision may have had on the wife and two elementary-school-aged children who survived him.

Finally, Rule #3 increases the pressure on poverty-and working-class families of all colors. Lack of opportunities for reasonably-paid employment can contribute to men's escalation of behavioral patterns that, they believe, serve to re-affirm their wounded masculinity. In other words, men who are struggling economically often become more domineering toward the women and children in their lives.

RULE

Be Self-Reliant!

Nick, a fifty-three-year-old French-Canadian, yearly experienced one-to-three-week-long periods during which he could barely drag himself out of bed, felt entirely worthless, and needed to argue himself out of committing suicide on an almost daily basis. Many years ago, a psychiatrist diagnosed Nick with bipolar affective disorder, and prescribed necessary medication to control the symptoms. The desolate stretches inevitably lifted, and Nick would be back to his old self again: cheerful, positive, and full of energy to share with his wife, fourteen-year-old daughter, and the whole world. He wrote reams of poetry, sang loudly to passers-by while strolling through lower Manhattan on his way to work, wrote thoughtful letters to the editors of local and national newspapers, and read voraciously. A captivating speaker and raconteur, he was a joy to be around. Three times during his life, however, his brilliance exploded into periods of dire stress for his family. On the most recent of these occasions, he had set off for work at the usual time, logged on (he worked as a securities trader) as the market opened and then mysteriously disappeared at some point during the afternoon.

He went missing from home and work for five days, after which his wife received a telephone call from the authorities in Montreal, Canada, reporting that Nick was hospitalized in a psychiatric ward there. He had arrived in the country four days earlier dressed in combat fatigues. At the airport, he seized the attention of all present by proclaiming through a bullhorn that he had urgent news from Che Guevara regarding an international terrorist plot that could only be foiled if he were put in charge of all Canadian armed forces immediately.

After a long and difficult ordeal, requiring Renee, Nick's wife of nineteen years, to fly to Montreal and escort Nick home, he once again refused to continue taking the medications that were prescribed for his mental illness. As he had done following previous manic episodes, Nick insisted that his vitamins and supplements, as well as the regimen of dietary, meditation, and exercise practices to which he attributed the previous three years of relative stability, were all that was necessary to ensure another extended period of mental health. People who struggle with mental health problems typically resist compliance with their prescribed treatment. It is likely that this dynamic, along with Nick's adherence to Rule #4, contributed to his refusal of medication. Renee had decided three years previously that she would leave Nick if he suffered another episode and thereafter refused psychiatric assistance. Reluctantly, she initiated divorce proceedings.

In another example, Todd and Christopher, a gay African-American couple who had lived together for ten years, encountered a crisis in their relationship after Todd lost his clerical job at a New York City media corporation. Fed up with the uncertainties of corporate employment, Todd embarked on his dream career as a work-from-home currency trader. Todd had received a severance package and was also eligible for unemployment insurance. He purchased a software trading application advertised on the internet and a new computer.

Christopher, a self-employed plumbing contractor, encouraged Todd to consult the financial planner and accountant who had helped him for years, offering to pay for a consultation with each professional. Christopher told Todd that he wanted him to have the best advice possible so he could plan his business and also make the best use of his personal finances. Todd thanked his partner but stressed his desire to "make it on my own."

Todd threw himself into his new work, spending at least twelve hours every day on the computer. While he mostly declined to talk about his progress, Todd's increasingly foul mood belied his lack of success.

Not only Christopher, but also the couple's closest friends, offered Todd advice and assistance. Julie, an accounting professional who had recently been downsized herself, advised Todd to seek part-time employment so he'd experience less financial pressure. Andrew, an interior designer who valued Todd's talent for identifying marketable antiques and paintings, offered Todd a part-time job. Todd continued his full-time devotion to trading.

Matters came to a head when Todd informed Christopher that he had nearly exhausted his savings, increased his debt to a point that frightened him, and could no longer contribute to shared living expenses. Christopher agreed to assist Todd financially only if he sought part-time employment and would see a couples therapist.

As these stories illustrate, even in the direst circumstances some men refuse to ask for and accept assistance. Rule #4 teaches boys and men to feel entitled to make decisions based solely upon their own perspectives and judgments, regardless of the impact upon others. It also teaches males to equate asking for help with failure and weakness. While the impact of Rule #4 upon important relationships can be catastrophic, less extreme problems are often brought on by a man's refusal to engage assistance. The challenge associated with Rule #4 calls for boys and men to realize that asking for help does not signify weakness. Quite the contrary, the willingness to ask for and accept help become vitally important life skills.

5

RULE

Be Aggressive!

Sylvia, a fifty-two-year-old Chinese-American woman, and Charles, her fifty-six-year-old Swiss-American husband, clashed after receiving the devastating news that their twenty-year-old daughter, Amber, had been diagnosed with a malignant ovarian tumor. Sylvia, sad and pensive, spent a great deal of time with Amber. Amber experienced her mother's behavior as love and concern, and felt greatly supported. Together, Sylvia and Amber agreed that it would make sense for Amber to move back home from her apartment and take a brief leave of absence from college while she underwent more tests and prepared to make decisions about her course of treatment. When they brought this suggestion to Charles he was outraged.

Angered by what he saw as his wife and daughter's surrender to the cancer, Charles told Amber that he did not want her to leave school. Furthermore, he demanded that she join his health club and work out with him every evening. He insisted that Amber and her mother "stop crying and thinking weak thoughts" as these actions were "inviting defeat." He also told Amber that he would interview her oncologist to make sure the doctor was "going after this tumor with everything we've got."

Amber felt dismissed and infantilized by her father's demands. She told him that she felt frightened and confused and needed time to think through all the new information that was before her.

"This isn't some kind of war game or marathon I need boot camp to get ready for, Dad. This is about trying to make the best decisions so I can take care of myself, live through this, and be well again."

Charles's intention was to get ready, aim, and fire with every weapon at his disposal. In trying to impose this approach, he ran roughshod over the sensibilities and contributions of his wife and daughter, and increased emotional distance at a time when togetherness and collaboration were desperately needed by all of them. If he had tempered this approach by first respecting their need to grieve and think through a variety of options, his energetic optimism might have made a wonderful contribution to the family's collaborative response.

A certain degree of aggression (or at least assertion) and toughness is not always a bad thing. Most conflicts or problems can be more constructively approached by a combination of means, however. Rule #5 entitles men facing relationship difficulties to respond with aggression. When aggression and toughness become the *first and only* tactics one applies, the results are rarely positive.

RULE

Be Dominant!

Closely connected to Rule #1 ("Don't act like a girl!") and Rule #5 ("Be aggressive!"), Rule #6 assigns men "head of the household" status within families, as well as positions of ultimate leadership within all other organizations. The worldwide impact of this rule can be seen in the enduring pattern of predominantly male leadership in government, business, educational, and religious institutions within our society, as in well as most societies across the world. Rule #6 teaches boys and men that power in relationships means being in a position to control other people. Power equals domination. I will discuss this and alternative notions of power more extensively in Chapter Four.

The family situation used to exemplify Rule #5 applies equally well to Rule #6. Charles presumes to dictate the course of actions he wants the family to follow. It is important to consider that Charles' attitude of entitlement to authority within the family may stand in marked contrast to his persona as an employee. Charles works as an actuary at a financial services firm. He would never presume to dictate any course of action to his supervisor. Instead, he respectfully defers to his supervisor and invites collaboration.

While this difference may seem contrary to Rule #6, it actually demonstrates a corollary of the rule—men generally respect their assigned level within the hierarchy of work and military organizations because they see compliance as a vehicle for ultimately gaining more power. Another way to state this corollary is, "Be a good soldier."

At the beginning of this chapter, I mentioned that the rules for male behavior reflect mainstream American values, i.e. middle and upper-middle class, predominantly white, predominantly heterosexual sensibilities. As the following example illustrates, while the rules originate within this most influential group, they shape attitudes and behavior across our society.

Alice Walker's novel, *The Color Purple,* celebrates the survival of African-American women who have endured incest, other forms of child abuse, domestic violence, and the viciousness of life in the Jim Crow South. The book (and the movie that followed) ignited a controversy within the community of African-American artists. Some writers, primarily men, vociferously attacked Walker. They argued that it was disrespectful and dangerous for her to write about such issues within the current racist social context because doing so contributed to the distorted picture that mainstream American society already held of African-American males. Walker's supporters countered that while struggling to eradicate racism it is also imperative for community members, male and female alike, to work together toward acknowledging and solving all social problems that exist within their communities, including male dominance and the sexual exploitation of women and girls by men. They found it unacceptable to avoid a problem because it is caused largely by men and suffered mostly by women.

RULE

Women Are For Sex!

"Baby, you know what I'm gonna do? I'm gonna put you over my shoulder, carry you into that bedroom of yours, and peel off your clothes with my teeth! Oh yeah, and you're gonna love it. I'm gonna lay you back on that bed, and climb on top of you," purred thirty-seven-year-old Matt into Gloria's ear. He placed his hand over hers. This was their third date and the first time he'd been invited into her home. After making dinner together in her kitchen, they had spent the evening watching a video. Now, he thought, she played hard to get.

Having tried for what seemed an eternity to convince Matt that their date was over and it was time for him to head home, Gloria stood at her front door with her right hand on the doorknob. She hoped that she'd be able to open the door and usher Matt out. For the past several minutes she had also been considering grabbing the phone and dialing 911 or rushing across the hall to seek help from a neighbor. She desperately wished it wouldn't come to that. Gloria paled as she felt Matt's hand on top of her own, restraining her from turning the doorknob.

"I'm serious, Matt, I want you to leave! I'm not kidding. You are making me *very* uncomfortable," Gloria stammered.

"Wow, you're really scared!" said Matt. He released her hand and took a half-step backwards. "I had no idea I was frightening you. Don't you know me better than that? You actually think I'd do something to hurt you? I'm really amazed."

"I want you to leave now," said Gloria. She opened the front door of her condo.

"But can't we talk about this? I don't want to leave on this kind of a note. Please let me reassure you. I feel terrible. Actually I'm also kind of insulted. I can't believe you would think I might hurt you!" Matt said.

"We can talk about it another time," said Gloria.

After closing the door behind him, she slumped against it and began to cry.

Most boys in our society experience their first sexual encounters with pornographic magazines, videotapes, or online images instead of with a real, physically present, human being. Pornography leads us to conceptualize partners as existing solely to gratify us, and always at our disposal. Pornographic images are airbrushed to perfection, never tired, not feeling well, preoccupied with other life priorities, or maybe just plain not interested. Once we've had our orgasm, we can just put the magazine or videotape aside and move on. Also, pornographic images never say "no." I should clarify: pornographic images may *pretend* to say "no," but that's always just a tease, and what they really mean is "yes."

Beginning our sexual lives in this way sets men up to experience sex as something we do for ourselves, mostly by ourselves. Sex may be enhanced by the physical (or maybe even just online "real time") presence of another person, but that's hardly a requirement. The goal of our sexual interests is to use an image that arouses us for our own gratification. Pornography also teaches that "real men" are ready for sex at all times, and that the pursuit of sex is rightfully one of life's main preoccupations.

Pornography promotes racist stereotypes—black women,

whores; black men, overly endowed rapists; Southeast Asian women, exotic tempresses with mysterious techniques for driving men wild. Each of these stereotypes reflects the enduring history of white men's sexual exploitation of people of color. White men systematically raped black women in this country for centuries. Stereotyping black women as insatiable and black men as rapists absolves white men through victim blaming. Nonetheless, these pornographic stereotypes continue to shape men's attitudes toward themselves and others.

Rule #7 teaches boys and men to feel entitled to receive sex from those whom we find sexually appealing. (For gay men, Rule #7 becomes "Men are for sex!") The idea of a mutually respectful, loving, and gratifying relationship with another human being as the optimum context for sex mystifies many men. In fact, even though we may be lucky enough to observe something close to this description in our parents' relationship and in other couple relationships, we often view this kind of closeness as a sexual turn-off. We see this type of connection as boring, stodgy, and drained of excitement. The real turn-on, many of us have come to believe, requires a partner who is perfect, new, and mysterious, interested mostly in sex, and, for all intents and purposes, disposable.

Men often spend their first intimate relationships, at great emotional and spiritual cost to their partners as well as themselves, confronting and trying to unlearn the fallacies of this pornographized vision of partnership. Some men resolve the dilemma by dislocating sex from other aspects of partnership, inviting heartbreaking conflicts for all involved. In one rather extreme example, I knew a man who dismissed his regular extra-relational sexual encounters as having no meaning and impact upon his "committed" relationship with his partner. When she stumbled upon evidence of these trysts, he self-assuredly explained to her that these sexual encounters were "the equivalent of tennis games scheduled with friends and have nothing to do with our relationship." Had his partner agreed to these "sporting events" in advance, his argument might have held more credibility.

RULE

Don't Be Gay!

Homophobia, fear or hatred toward gay men, lesbians, and bisexuals, remains one of the hallmarks of traditional masculinity. In fact, some gender theorists argue that mainstream ideas about male identity are based most fundamentally upon Rules #1 ("Don't act like a girl!") and #8. In other words, "real" men are supposed to be nothing like girls and one hundred percent heterosexual. Rule #8 contributes to hate crimes across a continuum of intensity and impact. These crimes include gay bashings that result in murder, such as what was done in 1998 to Matthew Shepherd in Laramie, Wyoming, along with self-hate crimes, like the many suicides committed by gay teens each year. Rule #8, as the following case illustrates, entitles men to despise people based upon sexual orientation, and this can tear families and communities apart.

Josh is a fifty-year-old white man. His family lineage includes people of German, Irish, and Native American ethnicity. He lives with his wife, Naomi, also fifty years old, and their two teenaged children in a small town outside Atlanta, Georgia. Josh is a leader within his Southern Baptist community of faith. Josh's mother, Sybil, lives across the street. Josh has two younger brothers, Tom, who is forty-seven and lives in New York City, and David, who is forty-four and lives in Tampa, Florida.

Tom and David are gay. This fact has never been discussed

openly within the family. Recently, Tom, who has lived with his partner for the past five years, decided to "come out" to his family. He sent a long eloquently written letter to his mother, two brothers, sister-in-law, niece, and nephew, revealing his sexual orientation. Tom hoped, as he stated in the letter, that his disclosure would remove blocks in communication and strengthen his connection to each family member.

The response he received was not what he expected. Tom had always spoken freely to his family members of his living arrangements with his partner, and close interactions with his partner's nine-year-old son, extended family, and ex-wife's family. Tom felt that coming out to his family would be more formality than anything else, knowing as he did that on at least one occasion his sister-in-law had fielded questions from her children regarding the likelihood of Tom and David being gay.

Josh responded to Tom's letter by telling him over the phone, "I think you are on the road to destruction and I don't want you to have any more contact with my children." He continued, "If you were to come home, I believe you would be at risk," refusing to clarify what "at risk" meant. Thereafter, Tom received an email from his other brother, David, stating that he believed Tom had destroyed the family by making this announcement. David concluded his email by saying he never wanted to see Tom again. Tom was baffled by this communication, as David is gay and this was not a secret between the two of them.

Sybil phoned Tom to tell him that his announcement was the worst thing that had ever happened to her, far worse, in fact, than the emotional and physical abuse she suffered at the hands of her husband, who finally left the family when Tom was eight years old. Sybil tearfully reminded Tom of several lines of scripture that her community believes certify homosexuality as an abomination. Tom's rebuttal, complete with scriptural references, fell upon deaf ears.

Tom began talking over the responses of his family members

with friends and his therapist. In addition to processing his own feelings, he grew increasingly concerned for his nineteen-year-old nephew, Jason. Tom had felt for several years that Jason might be gay and struggling to hold onto feelings of self-worth and integrity. Tom worried that Josh's response to Tom's coming out letter would make the young man feel even more isolated and despairing.

Rule #8 teaches males to be hostile toward gay and bisexual men, and to be self-loathing if we happen to be other than heterosexual ourselves. It also teaches us to remain emotionally distant from other men, lest we be taken for gay or bisexual.

Because none of us can entirely block out the ways of the world, let us assume that all men enact the rules described above to some degree. The same goes for the attitudes of entitlement the rules support. No matter how progressive and egalitarian-minded our parents may have been, no matter how emphatically each of us vows to resist the roles assigned by gender, race, class, and sexual orientation, daily life in our society continues to envelop each of us with its traditions and expectations. We cannot help but absorb some of them. The more we examine the rules of the male code, however, the more we empower ourselves to scrutinize the ideas about others and ourselves that are everywhere in the world around us. This fortifies us for making choices that are the difference between accepting and resisting patterns that threaten our relationships; we need this fortification because these choices arise frequently, every single day.

Society persists in assigning girls and women almost all of the work involved with building and maintaining relationships. One of the most significant entitlements our society has traditionally granted men is a pass on taking responsibility for their contributions to the difficulties that arise within intimate relationships. This is profoundly unfair. Acknowledging the rules of male behavior helps us remember that we are active participants within our intimate partnerships and empowers us to claim our fair share of responsibility for both the trials and triumphs.

✦ ✧ ✦ ACTION STEPS ✦ ✧ ✦
MEN

FOR EACH OF THE RULES PRESENTED IN THIS CHAPTER:

1. Describe a recent instance in which you felt pressured to conform.

2. List three things you can do next time that will help you resist conforming.

3. Follow through with these new "actions of resistance" at your next opportunity.

4. Note how other men respond when you resist conforming to the rule.

5. Note how resisting the rule benefits your most important relationships.

✦ ✧ ✦ ACTION STEPS ✦ ✧ ✦
WOMEN

FOR EACH OF THE RULES PRESENTED IN THIS CHAPTER:

1. Describe a recent instance in which you felt pressure to go along with or support that rule.

2. List three things you can do next time that will help you resist playing a supporting role.

3. Follow through with your resistance at the next available opportunity.

4. Note how men and women respond to you when you don't support the rule.

5. Note how your new behavior benefits your self-esteem and your most important relationships.

✦ ✧ ✦ **ACTION STEPS** ✦ ✧ ✦
COUPLES

FOR EACH OF THE RULES PRESENTED IN THIS CHAPTER:

1. Describe an instance when the rule had a negative impact upon your partnership.

2. Decide how each of you can act differently the next time one or both of you feels pressure to follow or support the rule.

3. Talk about how your new pattern of action will benefit your couple partnership.

4. Monitor each other. Praise your partner when you see them resisting the rule and let them know when you see them conforming.

4

Is My Partner
Listening-Impaired?

✦ ✧ ✦

Left unexamined and unchallenged, the male code runs like a script in the back of our minds, flashing directions that shape our attitudes and the choices we make every moment of our lives. The script supports male entitlement by reminding us that men are better than women and that relationship work, like other unpaid work, demands the attention of women more than men. Consequently, while many women have learned that successful partnership results from consistent listening, negotiation, compromise, and follow-through, most men decide that these responsibilities are simply not in their job description. Their decision guarantees problems, because successful couple relationships require *both* participants to participate in these activities.

Unfortunately, this may be news to many people, including some "relationship experts." The title of Laura Schlessinger's book, *The Proper Care and Feeding of Husbands,* evokes an image of what results when men and women decide that it is acceptable for men to refrain from being active relationship partners. Asked during an interview whether *The Proper Care and Feeding of Wives* was forthcoming, Schlessinger responded, "Nope . . . what women accept or reject is largely the guiding force for what men will and won't do." She assigns all of the responsibility for a man's behavior to his female partner. Real intimate partnerships, on the other hand, require that *both* participants:

+ listen to and remember their partner's words
+ acknowledge and express their feelings
+ respond empathically to feelings expressed by their partner
+ take each other seriously
+ raise concerns that are troubling them
+ listen non-defensively to concerns raised by their partner
+ negotiate in good faith
+ reliably follow through with agreed-upon changes
+ consistently behave in a manner that inspires trust

When one partner decides to evade any of these responsibilities, the relationship may persist in the form of an enabling, caregiving, or hostage situation, but none of these should be mistaken for an intimate partnership.

The case description that follows illustrates one of the all-too-familiar roads to relationship crisis that results when a man unquestioningly adheres to the male code and the attitude of entitlement it supports. As you read this case, look for the ways that the man's loyalty to the code prevents him from being an effective relationship partner. Note where his lack of active listening and follow-through contribute to the couple's difficulties. Ask yourself, "Why is each partner deciding to listen or not listen to their partner?"

Henry and Jackie, a white middle-class couple in their mid-thirties with no children, came to see me for a consultation. Henry, a mid-level manager in a pharmaceutical firm, and Jackie, a head nurse in a neo-natal intensive care unit, had been married for ten years. In shock, with eyes wide open like he'd just seen a ghost, Henry launched into his story even before we had all sat down. "I can't believe this is happening! Everything seemed to be pretty much fine as far as I could tell until last Saturday morning." He thought for a moment and added, "I guess, in looking back, I may have felt that there was a little distance between us, but no huge problem." Henry continued, "I couldn't believe it, though, when Jackie told me she wanted a divorce. I just couldn't believe it! I kept asking her what I had done wrong and what I could do to make things better. But she didn't even want to talk about it! She said there was nothing I could do to change her mind."

Jackie, shaking her head from side to side and frowning, jumped in. "From the way he tells it, you'd think I clobbered him out of thin air!" she said looking at Henry with tears in her eyes. Hastily outstretching both open palms in a gesture of exasperation, she continued, "How many times did I ask you to spend a little time with me; you know—go out to a nice dinner or just sit and talk? Whenever you did something with me, you made me feel like I had nagged you into it. I always ended up feeling like I was stealing you away from one of your precious cable sporting events or some other damn TV show!"

Jackie held her shaking head in her hands briefly, and then once again fixed her eyes on Henry's. She drew a deep breath, steadied herself in her chair, and continued. "How many times have I wanted you to just show some interest and have a conversation about things going on at my job? I listened to everything that went on at your office. I knew everybody's name and exactly how you felt about them. You've never shown anything close to that kind of interest in my life! When I pressed you about that kind of stuff, you told me something about not being a 'touchy-feely' sort of guy. You always seemed pretty damned touchy-feely when it came to stuff that was important to you!"

As Jackie sighed and took a deep breath, I found myself reflecting upon the many times I'd heard men say they aren't "touchy- feely." I wondered what it will take for men to recognize that paying attention to feelings, one's own as well as those of one's partner, is part of the deal when you commit to an intimate partnership. It's not negotiable for men and it's not negotiable for women. It is one of the requirements of intimacy.

Jackie continued, "There have been all sorts of other problems. For one, you always wanted to initiate sex but were never interested on the few occasions when I tried to start things off. I've told you a million times that it's pretty hard to feel interested when I'm treated like a stranger until we fall into bed. I asked you so many times to go to counseling with me, starting at least eight years ago. You told me I was being too sensitive, that things weren't so bad. One way or another, you made it perfectly clear that you weren't willing to participate. You always left me feeling like you thought I was asking you for a lot, and all I wanted was some emotional contact. I just wanted to feel like you were with me, like you cared about me!"

Henry said, "Of course I care about you! How could you think otherwise? I live with you. I sleep in the same bed with you every night. I love you so much. I can't believe you don't know that." Distressed, he shuddered and folded his arms tightly.

Looking to me, Jackie concluded. "About a year ago, I guess, I just decided to stop begging and started dealing realistically with what was going on. I started spending more time with my friends, reading more, and doing things that made me feel more content. I started paying more attention to what I'm interested in, what I want out of life. I was through banging my head against the wall, trying to get blood from this stone of a marriage. When I told him I wanted to separate, I pretty much figured that he felt the same way and that it would be a relief for both of us. Boy, was I surprised by his reaction! He was the one who called you to set up this appointment. I'm here because he asked me to come with him, but I'm one hundred percent clear on my decision to leave the marriage."

While the details vary, the relationship pattern in this example is common. One partner, usually the woman within heterosexual couples, explains during their first visit that she's been trying to get her partner's attention for years by sharing her concerns as honestly and lovingly as possible, suggesting things they can try to do differently or that they get professional help. Only when she gives up and says that she's ready to move out does he pay attention. Then he begs her to join him in couples therapy. For their part, the men in these couples often cannot remember a single complaint being raised until "she dropped the bomb that she was leaving." Like Henry, they report that things in the relationship seemed fine up until that point.

Is this pattern the result of a communication problem? I pose this question first because many people, including many therapists, would see it as such. Well, yes and no. In none of the cases that I've seen has either partner had an undiagnosed hearing impairment, neurological problem, or a difficulty understanding the language they share. The basic machinery that makes communication possible worked. Furthermore, the woman's complaints had been raised directly and repeatedly, so it's not about a lack of willingness to be up front and expressive. The problem does have a great deal to do with a particular aspect of communication, however. That vital aspect of communication is listening. One party within the relationship isn't listening to the other.

But is this a difficulty, an impairment of some kind, over which Henry and many other men have little or no control? If such were the case, we would find the same problem disrupting not just this relationship, but each of his other relationships as well. It would be important therefore to make the following sorts of inquiries. Does Henry demonstrate a similar listening problem in his relationships with other important people in his life—his manager at work, his friends, and his father—for example? Generally, this isn't the case. What we're more likely to observe is that the listening problem experienced by Henry (and the other men who find themselves in similar predicaments) is exquisitely selective in nature, visiting only their partner relationship. This means that the men in question *make a decision* to refrain from listening to their partners.

From his partner's perspective, it isn't always blatantly evident that the man is not listening. He usually gives the appearance of listening when she speaks to him. Thereafter, however, he doesn't follow through with changes they've agreed upon or doesn't remember their conversation when she references it. Feeling ignored, his partner eventually gives up on words and moves into action instead. Sometimes she has an affair or announces her decision to leave the relationship, but she often chooses less extreme measures, such as moving into a different bedroom, decreasing the amount of time she spends at home, leaving on a weekend trip with friends without previous notice, or no longer doing his laundry and other housework. This is when the message makes an impact.

What accounts for a man's decision to stop listening to his partner? Does it mean he doesn't love her? Well, yes and no. In most cases, the partners involved express great affection and concern for each other. They generally say that they *feel* love for each other, that the problem is something other than that. Sometimes, as in Jackie's case, the neglected partner, at wits' end and ready to leave, says the love she once felt has eroded or that she has "fallen out of love." Even though the problem adversely affects the feelings experienced by both partners, however, they don't usually describe it as a failure of love.

But if your definition of love includes *loving action* as one of the guiding principles, then Henry has indeed failed to show

Jackie love. How can we say we love another person and at the same time disregard their words that tell us we're causing pain?

The problem proves even more fundamental than a question of love, however. At the center of the problem lies disrespect. The male code teaches men that they can choose to disrespect women, but, more specifically and perversely, they are most free to disrespect the women who are closest to them. A man's "listening problem" often intensifies after a relationship commitment begins. Many women remember the problem starting after the couple became engaged, moved in together, or married.

Bear in mind the certainty of choice. The point confuses many people. They excuse a man from his responsibility to be a respectful listener, and, more broadly, a respectful partner in all areas of the relationship. Please note: this is a point about which many marriage and family therapists, psychologists, psychiatrists, and family court judges *seem* profoundly confused. They excuse men for deciding not to listen or for behaving even more disrespectfully toward women in some other manner. In fact, there are books—series of books even—which argue that the responsibilities men and women bear toward each other within relationships need not be balanced and fair. Laura Schlessinger's work, mentioned earlier, provides one example. Psychologist John Gray has made a fortune selling the idea that it is *natural* for men and women to operate so differently that one is wise to imagine that the sexes originated on two different planets. He suggests numerous strategies that encourage women to accommodate themselves to men's disrespectful behavior.

While human differences, including gender, ethnicity, race, sexual orientation, age, and socioeconomic class, need to be acknowledged and examined in order to improve our understanding of many patterns within relationships, such aspects of identity should never be accepted as a justification for bad behavior. In other words, I'm asking you to refuse to accept nonsense explanations that encourage women to continue doing more of the work within relationships than men. I'm asking you to dig deeper, using principles of fairness and equality as your guiding light.

Let's assume that people of all genders carry an equal amount of responsibility within their partner relationships. This means that every time one partner initiates communication with the other, that second partner faces decisions about whether or not to pay attention, listen respectfully, carry on a dialogue, and follow through with any agreed-upon courses of action. The key word in the previous sentence is decisions. Making a decision involves a moment of personal responsibility in which we make a choice and thereafter follow through.

What factors influence our decisions about whether to demonstrate respect to another person by paying attention, actively listening to what they have to say, and then following through on joint decisions? Human behavior follows patterns. We can gain insight into a confusing relationship pattern by examining other situations in which a similar pattern exists. In this case, we're considering relationships in which listening and understanding flow in only one direction despite the fact that both parties interact continuously, speak the same language, and are capable of hearing and understanding. Where else do we see this besides intimate partnerships? The examples below have relevance not only for our current discussion but also for topics addressed within subsequent chapters.

White Americans and African-Americans have been relating to one another for centuries. African-Americans resisted the holocaust of slavery in a multitude of ways, clearly and consistently communicating their demands for human rights. The majority of white Americans and the United States government chose not to listen to these demands. Instead, the government initiated and legitimized the violence necessary to perpetuate slavery and the system of racial inequality that persisted thereafter.

Laborers in the manufacturing, railroad, and mining industries during the 19th and 20th centuries consistently and clearly communicated to their employers their demands for safe working environments and reasonable wages. Those who owned and managed these industries responded with mercenaries and government troops whose orders were to restore quiet, whatever the cost.

In each case, only when those whose voices were being brutally dismissed organized into movements—strong enough to demand their rights in a manner that was disruptive to the lives of their oppressors—did the pattern begin to shift. Why did it take disruptive action to force one group to begin listening to the other with some degree of respect?

The answer has to do with power. When a gross imbalance in power exists, those who hold more power often decide to disregard the voices of those who hold less. They do this because they can; it works (at least in the short term), and nobody can make them do otherwise. When I speak of power, I mean all the forms related to the particular relationship. These often include political, economic, physical, emotional, and spiritual power. Knowledge of local topography, wisdom, language skills, and resourcefulness are other forms of power. If the overall balance of power shifts (as it did in both of the examples mentioned above), and those who have for a very long time decided to dismiss and/or suppress the voices of their relationship partners suddenly find it in their interest to begin listening, negotiating, and accepting change, then the relationship moves toward increased fairness.

The women's movement provides an example that even more closely resembles what went on between Henry and Jackie. Women in this country gained access to full rights of citizenship

only by organizing into collectives that demanded equal treatment under the law. Strikes, protest marches, and coalition-
building elevated their political and economic power. Collective
moral vision optimized their emotional and spiritual power.
When their power exceeded the power of those who sought to
dismiss their claims, they prevailed.

Do I mean to suggest that Jackie's announcement that she had
decided to leave Henry was equivalent to a strike, equal rights
demonstration, or protest march? That's exactly what I'm suggesting. When Jackie announced that she was leaving Henry, it
wasn't that Henry simultaneously experienced a miraculous
remission in his undiagnosed hearing problem and was able for
the first time to listen to the words she was speaking. Rather,
Jackie's declaration caused Henry to recognize that the balance
of power in the relationship had shifted. Jackie's request for a
divorce signaled that she now had the power to *demand* that
Henry take her seriously. Her request made it clear that she had
the emotional, spiritual, and economic power necessary to establish an authentic life for herself as a single person in response to
Henry's unwillingness to meet her needs as a partner. Jackie's
announcement dislodged Henry's entitlement to behave disrespectfully toward her. Suddenly, he was all ears.

Power sets the foundation for relationships more than communication, love, and respect. Misuse of power caused Henry
and Jackie's relationship crisis, and it causes relationship difficulties for many other couples as well. To the list of required activities for intimate partners mentioned at the beginning of this
chapter, I make two additions. Intimate partners must also:

✦ acknowledge the dynamics of power within their
   relationship
✦ refrain from misusing their power

The tragedy of this chapter's case example is that such painful situations seem, in hindsight, to be entirely preventable. After all, paying attention to the person one professes to love hardly seems like an unreasonable expectation. So, why are such simple aspects of intimate partnership so profoundly difficult for many people, most of them male? One of the main reasons, I believe, is our dogged unwillingness to confront the issue of power within intimate relationships directly. We can't begin to change a pattern without facing it head on. The following chapters do just that.

✦ ✧ ✦ ACTION STEPS ✦ ✧ ✦
MEN

1. Identify at least two women other than your partner whom you trust and respect.

2. Describe the theme of this chapter for each woman—that men generally listen less responsibly to women, and, more generally, that most people listen less well to individuals with less power than themselves.

3. Listen very carefully to her response after you ask each woman to describe at least one experience in which she felt a man was listening less respectfully to her than he would to another man.

4. Write a list of adjectives that describe how each woman felt when disrespected in this manner.

5. Share this exercise and your resulting list with at least one man whom you trust and respect. Discuss with him what you will do differently as a result.

✦ ✧ ✦ ACTION STEPS ✦ ✧ ✦
WOMEN

1. Discuss with two close women friends the pattern that finds men not listening as well to women as they do to other men, and, more generally, people listening less carefully to individuals with less power than themselves. Share examples from each of your personal experiences.

2. Brainstorm five specific responses that each of you can enact the next time you recognize that a man's not really listening. Examples include:

    ◇ Writing down your next words, rather than speaking them, and handing him the paper.
    ◇ Switching to a foreign language that he doesn't understand.
    ◇ Resorting to mime.
    ◇ Following through on an agreed-upon plan without reminding him—even after you recognize that he wasn't paying attention.
    ◇ The last option allows consequences that may help him learn to pay better attention, such as missing an appointment or family event.

3. Agree that you will take one of these actions rather than saying, "You're not listening to me."

4. Check in with these friends within two weeks and periodically thereafter to share how you're each following through and the resulting male behavior.

✦ ✧ ✦ **ACTION STEPS** ✦ ✧ ✦
COUPLES

1. Review the list of things that loving partners do for one another from the beginning of this chapter:

    ⬦ listen to and remember their partner's words.

    ⬦ acknowledge and express their feelings.

    ⬦ respond empathically to feelings expressed by their partner.

    ⬦ take one another seriously.

    ⬦ raise concerns that are troubling them.

    ⬦ listen non-defensively to concerns raised by their partner.

    ⬦ negotiate in good faith.

    ⬦ reliably follow through with agreed-upon changes.

    ⬦ consistently behave in a manner that inspires trust.

2. Discuss each bullet point and come to an agreement regarding whether or not you believe it accurately describes a responsibility of partnership. Feel free to delete some of my points and add others of your own.

3. Post your list as a reminder on your refrigerator, dresser, or somewhere else that's visible.

4. Make a point to praise your partner when you notice them taking actions that appear on the list. You may also decide to reference the list during your weekly partnership meetings (from Chapter Two's Action Steps for Couples).

5

A Closer Look at Power

✦ ✧ ✦

The most important thing to pay attention to when you're trying to make sense of what's going on in a relationship isn't communication, and it isn't love—it's power. Keep this idea firmly in mind, and you'll be way ahead of just about everybody else, including most psychologists, psychiatrists, therapists, and other "relationship experts." Love, communication, mutual respect, shared interests, and lots of other things are important, but taking a look at the balance of power between partners provides the most informative starting point for understanding everything else that's going on.

The balance of power between partners shapes nearly every aspect of a relationship, not only who speaks and is listened to versus who speaks and goes unheard, as was discussed within Chapter Four. The power balance also affects:

+ how joint decisions are reached
+ the extent to which each partner remembers the details of the other's life: their likes, dislikes, dreams, achievements, and disappointments

- ✦ who gets to define whether or not a concern is a problem that the couple needs to address
- ✦ the extent to which each partner claims time and space for solitary activities
- ✦ who does the least pleasant household tasks

Power is an invisible force that contributes to the structure of every relationship: invisible because many of its indications are so ever-present that most people overlook their significance, just as we overlook the air we breathe. This chapter spotlights the ways that power operates within personal relationships, raising this important dynamic out of the shadows and into the light of critical consciousness. First, we'll define the term.

TWO VISIONS OF POWER

Within most societies, power generally means the power of domination: the power to control resources and direct the activities of people. The male code described within Chapter Three teaches this understanding of power. It is the traditional power of a man as "head of household" and the power that a CEO holds over those who work for him. The command structure within most military organizations provides another example. This vision of power leads us to approach human differences of all kinds— gender, skin color, religion, ethnicity, and language—with "ranking questions," questions that establish and maintain hierarchy. Examples include:

- ✦ Which is stronger / weaker?
- ✦ Which is better / worse?
- ✦ Which is right / wrong?
- ✦ Which is sane / insane?

+ Which is healthy / unhealthy?
+ Which is moral / immoral?

Accordingly, we organize our understanding of the world into hierarchies of strength, goodness, correctness, sanity, healthfulness, and morality. We are left with a worldview that has little room for equality across differences.

An alternative definition envisions power as "shared responsibility" and "power with" instead of "domination over." Within this definition, power becomes the responsibility to organize and nurture oneself and others for the benefit of all concerned. This notion of power rejects domination in favor of love. It presumes equality and coexistence rather than inequality and the right to control others. When encountering people who are different from themselves, those who hold this definition of power ask questions such as:

+ "What can we learn from one another?"
+ "How can we help one another?"
+ "What can we accomplish together?"

The structure of biological systems provides an example. The brain does not command and control the other organ systems, but rather orchestrates their collaborative functioning in order to facilitate health for the entire organism.

This chapter pays attention mostly to power as domination because that, unfortunately, remains the primary expression of power within our society. I'll help you identify how the power of domination and control works within daily life by discussing a number of case examples from social situations both public and private. Analogies from the world around couple relationships, as we've seen in the last chapter, can help us make sense of similar patterns operating within intimate partnerships. *Keep in mind that the public and private worlds continuously influence and reflect one another.*

The chapter's final case example introduces a couple who demonstrate the second vision of power described above. Theirs is the power of mutual responsibility and collaboration: the power of love. *Resisting power as domination and embracing the power of love is the key to resolving many relationship difficulties.* Later sections of the book, starting with Chapter Nine, provide guidelines for making this happen.

The following section examines how aspects of our identities contribute to the balance of power within relationships.

THE LINKS BETWEEN IDENTITY AND POWER

Some people consider gender, race, and sexual orientation entirely personal characteristics because these aspects of ourselves reside at the heart of our identities, and therefore are arguably personal and private. But in the "power as domination" world in which we live, these aspects of ourselves link us to some people and differentiate us from others in ways that very publicly establish elements of our personal power. You've probably heard the saying, "The personal is political." Let's take a look at how it works.

Every piece of our identity either adds to or compromises the amount of power we bring into any given social situation. By "pieces of our identity" I mean aspects of ourselves such as:

+ our gender
+ our skin color
+ our financial resources
+ our sexual orientation
+ our age

+ our state of health or disability
+ our educational background
+ our social class background
+ our network of family and friends
+ our profession
+ the languages we are able to speak
+ the accent with which we speak English
+ our skill at articulating thoughts and feelings
+ the talents we possess
+ our spirituality
+ our religion
+ the secrets we hold
+ our physical attractiveness
+ our size and strength

The power (or lack thereof) connected to our particular mix of identity characteristics gives each of our encounters with other people a complex and dynamic footing. The following section provides illustrations.

RECOGNIZING POWER
AND PRIVILEGE IN ACTION

Two men, one black and one white, arrive at a street corner together after concluding their luncheon meeting, say their good-byes, and start hailing cabs. A cab immediately stops to pick up the white man. Before the black man gets his cab, however, five other white people arrive and are successful in securing theirs. Drawn from personal experiences described by entertainers Danny Glover and Harry Belafonte on a CNN television report, this example shows white privilege in action. The white people act out their privilege when, one after another, they get in their cabs while the black man is passed by. *Privilege is an advantage one gains by having human characteristics that identify one as a member of a powerful community.*

Notice the complexity here. The black man may benefit from the privileges typically granted men when he is at home with his wife and children. He may behave and be treated in ways that affirm his position of authority, but white privilege trumps male privilege when he's on a street corner seeking a cab. *The power and privilege each of us holds vary across settings.*

Notice also that not one of the white people pays attention to the disparity in treatment between themselves and the black businessman. *We usually take our privileges for granted.* The black man, on the other hand, is likely to be well aware of the discrimination directed toward him. *We are usually keenly aware of discrimination directed toward us.*

This is the way it works with all of our privileges, not just those connected to race. Most of us are painfully aware of the privileges denied us, but far less clear about those granted us. It's not difficult to look upward into the power hierarchy and see what others are receiving, but we're not. It's often very uncomfortable, however, to look downward to see our advantages over others. *Recognizing their privilege, however, is a key starting point for men who want to make important positive changes in their relationships.*

I benefit from many privileges. From the moment of my birth, when I was swathed in blue and presented to others as male, I was unwittingly granted membership into the world's most powerful society, the "white male community." While gifts of nature got me in the door—white skin and a penis—that was just the beginning when it came to developing a male identity. From there on, virtually everybody I met helped me learn the rules of the male code.

My "male training" was ongoing, an endless stream of small interactions every day. For example, I vividly remember one afternoon when I was nine years old and playing a game of tag with friends in my backyard. My mom and dad came outside to call me in for dinner. My dad loved the fact that I was a fast runner and relentlessly competitive. As I raced past my parents chasing after one of my friends, I heard my father proudly remark to my mother, "Look at that kid go—he's all boy!" There could be no better compliment. Even by that age I knew unquestioningly how important and powerful it was to be male.

I was also learning how important and powerful it was to be white. In school I was taught that white men were the thinkers and doers who made civilization happen. All of my history, science, mathematics, and storybooks made that clear, as did a look at any of the television programs, newspapers, or magazines that were available to me. Being "all boy" and white meant I was in the very best club. If my family had been wealthy, that would have been even better, but I knew that middle-class was still a relatively powerful place to be.

With every passing year, I took the rules of Chapter Three (What Patriarchy Teaches Men) more into myself, incorporating them into my personality and manner of presenting myself to the world because those around me rewarded me for doing so. They granted me the privileges afforded white males from middle- or upper-class backgrounds. These included being listened to with special attention, affirming my hope that I might reasonably aspire to positions of leadership and achievement, and overall confirming my significance as a person.

I know now that these experiences were privileges because if I had been female, a person of color, or a person who presented himself in a manner that was effeminate or otherwise non-traditional for a male, I would not have enjoyed the same treatment. Mainstream America confers a multitude of privileges upon those who happen to be male, white, heterosexual, "able-bodied," and from middle- or upper-class backgrounds.

Privilege fuels a person's attitude of entitlement. Entitlement, first mentioned in Chapter Two, is the expectation that one's needs, wants, ideas, and aspirations should be given first priority consideration by others. The power and privilege promised males in our society convince us that we are entitled to dominate women and children. For a reminder of the ways that men often demonstrate their entitlement, refer to the examples in Chapter Two.

Gaining critical consciousness about our power and privilege prepares us to make informed decisions regarding whether or not we'll continue behaving in an entitled and dominating manner. Taking on this challenge empowers men who want to improve their relationships with others. When we go along unquestioningly with the privileges granted us at the expense of others, we practice power as domination. When we acknowledge and begin to dismantle our participation in these privileges, we take steps toward practicing the power of love. Please take a few moments to identify several aspects of your identity that gain you a degree of power and privilege. Use the list that starts on page 35 under the heading "The links between identity and power" as a reference.

PERSONAL PARTICIPATION IN POWER, PRIVILEGE, AND DOMINATION

Each of us moves through the world with a complex mix of identity affiliations, some of which are associated with power and privilege, and others of which fall on the downside of the ranking questions mentioned earlier in this chapter. There are times when each of us is likely to practice domination, and there are times when we are likely to be on the receiving end of it, facing discrimination.

For example, I am privileged by my status as an able-bodied

white male of middle-class background, but I risk suffering discrimination whenever I decide to "out" myself as a gay man. I out
myself when I reveal that my intimate partnership is with
another man. For example:

- when I'm buying flowers and the cashier says, "Your
  wife sure is going to be happy when you give her
  these," and I reply, "Yup, my wife, Tim, sure is a
  lucky guy."
- when I display family pictures in my office that
  include my partner.
- when I give my partner a goodbye kiss before he
  gets on the train to go to work.

Because there is potential for danger in doing these things,
outing myself as a gay person engages risks that heterosexual
people, who out themselves continuously, never have to consider.

The mix of privilege and discrimination that we've learned to
associate with a number of identity aspects shapes the way we
participate in every relationship with others, within both the
public world and our most intimate relationships.

You and I are involved in a relationship as you read this book.
I decided not to reveal my gay identity to you until you reached
this page because negative attitudes toward gay people are so
prevalent that I feared you might decide not to read any further
if I outed myself earlier on. I decided that it would be better for
us to get further into our discussion before revealing this part
of myself.

Now let me ask you a question. Did learning that I'm gay
change your experience of our relationship in any manner?
Please be honest with yourself about this. If so, and the change
you notice is a distancing one, it's likely you've come face to
face with your heterosexism. Heterosexism is the system that

grants power and privilege to heterosexual people at the expense of others. It's the presumption that everybody you meet is heterosexual and that heterosexual people are more "normal," credible, and valuable than people with other sexual orientations. You're experiencing it if you find yourself wondering things like "How can a gay man be a father?" or "How can a gay man be an authority on intimate relationships between men and women?"

As is the case with sexism and racism, it's hard to avoid buying into heterosexism when you live in our society. It doesn't say anything bad about your character, therefore, if such is the case for you. What it means is that you, like most of us (including me), must work to recognize your own power and privilege, and try to interrupt the tendencies toward domination that come along with them.

Whether or not the revelation of my gay identity changed your relationship to me in the ways mentioned above, I'd like you to imagine for a moment that it did. Imagine that it caused you to question the validity of my ideas and suggestions, that it caused you to devalue me as a person. This shift in your attitude would be similar to what the male code teaches boys and men of all colors and sexual orientations to do in their relationships with girls and women. Heterosexism, sexism, and racism operate in this way, teaching us to overvalue some people and undervalue others—to grant power and privilege to some at the expense of others, affecting every encounter we have with other people, including those within our most intimate relationships. This is the essence of power as domination, exactly what we want to pay attention to so we can work toward eliminating our participation in it. The next section provides additional examples in an effort to shed more light on the way power works.

MORE EXAMPLES OF POWER, PRIVILEGE, AND DISCRIMINATION IN ACTION

I was a faculty member at a family therapy institute whose client population includes a number of families for whom domestic violence is an issue. Some years back, members of the institute's clinical team regularly attended family court days at the county courthouse. We habitually occupied the same, or approximately the same, seats in the courtroom. Juanita and Pilar, both of whom are dark-skinned Latinas; Miriam, who is Iranian-American; Shawnisse, who is African-American; and Linda and I, both of whom are white, would alternate in attendance so that we'd usually have at least three representatives from the institute present.

Judges Mills and Cross, when hearing from men who were our court-mandated clients, would regularly look to us and say, "Well, as we have faculty from the Family Therapy Institute present with us today, I'm going to ask them to fill me in on your attendance and progress." The one of us who had the most knowledge of the case would then briefly comment. Also, at the beginning of their court sessions, as either judge entered the courtroom, he would often nod and say hello to our group. Both judges were middle-aged white men.

Over several months, we began to recognize a disturbing pattern. Whenever Linda or I was present, the judge would recognize our group by nodding to us upon entry and calling on us for input. When neither Linda nor I was present, however, the judges would not seem to recognize those faculty who were present. On several of those occasions Judge Mills commented, "I wish there were staff from the Family Therapy Institute here but it appears there are none present." Juanita, Pilar, Miriam, or Shawnisse would then raise her hand, and the judge would offer a brief apology, and invite her to speak.

Why was it that the judges recognized Linda and me but not the other faculty? Neither Judge Mills nor Judge Cross had any prior connection to Linda or me, so it wasn't that they simply were more familiar with us. It also wasn't the case that Linda and I spoke more regularly to the judges than the other team members who attended court, so we couldn't have formed a significantly stronger impression because of having had more to say. Instead, it makes sense to conclude that the judges recognized and remembered us because we are white.

Power often works this way within relationships. There was nothing overtly hostile or rude about Judge Mills's and Judge Cross's disregard for the faculty members of color. Neither man actively insulted these women. The discrimination was expressed more subtly than that. In fact, if the judges were asked to comment on this pattern, it is unlikely that they would recognize the issue as their own. Instead, they might very well attribute the difference to other factors, maybe even describing those raising the issue as overly sensitive. *Power often works this way within relationships.*

Consider the issue of "nagging," for example. When a woman raises concerns but her partner ignores her, what is she likely to do? She's likely to repeat those concerns, and repeat them more emphatically. After she succeeds in getting her partner's attention, is he likely to reflect upon his lack of listening? Will he see it as male entitlement and domination for which he needs to take responsibility? Is he likely to apologize, and then pay attention to the concern that she's raising? In some cases, maybe, but it's more likely that he will decide that the problem is hers. He's likely to label that problem "nagging."

Think about what it means in terms of personal power to be recognized, remembered, and invited to speak by a judge within a court of law, one of the most significant forums within civil society. The visibility and recognition granted Linda and me because of our whiteness came from privilege. Power often shows itself within our most personal relationships in the form of similar privileges. Consider the way men often expect their partners to remember the names, positions, and relationships at their workplace. It is a privilege that the details of a man's workplace connections be remembered by his woman partner because men rarely reciprocate this attention.

By the way, please resist the temptation to file the story of Judge Mills and Judge Cross away as a peculiar case of rogue judges practicing racism. Isolating this particular story may help you feel better for the moment but this path leads away from the truth. Instead, try to recognize this example of power in action as one that can help you gain insight into the many ways power shapes all relationships. The following example should prove similarly instructive.

At an annual conference of the American Family Therapy Academy (AFTA) several years ago, I attended a presentation given by three white, female university professors. Their topic centered on differences in student behavior toward faculty based upon the faculty members' gender. The three described patterns they had observed over the course of several years, including the tendency of students to open the closed office doors of women professors, often without even knocking, but consistently respect the closed doors of male faculty members. Other patterns included expectations that women professors would be more readily available than men, and that the grades given by women were negotiable. One of the women, whose husband taught in the same family therapy department as she, told the following story. She said that on one occasion when her office door was closed a young woman student whom she had never met burst in upon her. The student announced, "I have to speak with Dr. Brunner (the woman faculty member's husband), but his door is closed, can you please ask him if he has time to see me?"

As the group began discussing this pattern, an elderly white man, one of the founders of the family therapy field, spoke to the presenters. "I don't think this is so much about gender as it is about the way you each present yourselves to others as individuals. Each of you seems to be such a warm, open kind of person. As you're speaking to us here, I'm experiencing you as very approachable. I think this aspect of yourself may be more what's bringing the students in so close to you than the fact that you are women. Could this be so?"

A middle-aged African-American man shook his head in disagreement. "Let me ask you something," he said to the presenters, "Are there any faculty members in your department who are people of color?"

The women looked at one another. Shaking their heads, one responded, "No."

"I didn't think so," the man said. He continued, "In my family therapy department there are a number of faculty members of color and we note a similar pattern to what you're describing, but it's a lot worse. For example, I can't tell you the number of times I've opened my office door to find a white student using my computer. My office door was closed, I wasn't even around, and these kids decided to help themselves to my computer! This is an experience shared by my colleagues of color. The last time it happened I was so exasperated that I just came right out with it. I said to the student, 'Let me ask you a question, would you just walk right in and start using my office equipment if I were a white professor?'"

After a pause, he turned to the elderly man whose question had brought him into the discussion. "I think it may be unsettling for some people to accept that race, gender, and other characteristics play a role in shaping the way people treat one another, particularly when it comes to things like the assumptions we make about our rights to others' time, attention, and property, but the sooner we all start looking this issue in the eye, the sooner we're going to do something to change it."

POWER, PRIVILEGE, AND DISCRIMINATION INSIDE COUPLE RELATIONSHIPS

Janice and Raul

Early in my family therapy training, several trainees and I observed a therapy session from behind a one-way mirror. The clients were a white couple, Janice and Raul, in their early forties whose marriage was in crisis after Janice's discovery of the fact that her husband had made a major investment, using joint funds, without even discussing the matter with her. The couple now faced a financial crisis. After the discovery, Raul begged his wife's forgiveness. He said that he wanted desperately to rebuild the marriage.

As the session got underway, Janice stated unequivocally that she wanted Raul to move out of the couple's home for a period of at least three months. This, she said, would give her time to begin to grieve and reassess the marriage without the everyday pressures of the relationship. Janice said this was the only way she would consider a reconciliation, and if Raul did not agree, she had decided that she would need to leave the relationship.

Raul seemed to have an impossible time making sense of what Janice was telling him. He repeatedly said, "But if we separate, then the marriage is over, so what's the difference?"

Janice told the therapist, a young white woman, that she couldn't seem to make Raul understand that she absolutely needed some space to deal with her feelings about what he had done. "He isn't listening to me. He keeps saying that separating will mean the marriage is over because that's the way that *he* sees it. There's nothing I can do about the way he feels, but I want to be true to my own feelings as well. If he really loves me the way he says he does, then he'll get this clear and give me some space."

It was becoming clear to those of us in the viewing room that neither the therapist nor Janice was making headway with Raul. Suddenly, a woman trainee remarked, "We should send a man in there. He'll listen to another man." Being the only man in the group, I was elected.

I walked into the room, sat down next to Raul, and said, "It seems, Raul, like the choice that will make Janice feel most comfortable right now is to plan a separation. You say you want to rebuild the marriage so it seems reasonable for you to strongly consider what Janice needs. As Janice said, a separation will help her sort through how she feels and what she'd like to see happen next."

Raul fixed his eyes on mine, and then he nodded his head into his hands and cried. After he regained his composure, I had a conversation with him about the importance of a man listening to the words his partner speaks and valuing them. I described how men typically decide to discount what their female partners have to say and how they feel, and challenged him to start paying as much attention to her words as he paid to mine. After I returned to the viewing room, the original therapist continued leading the session, and the couple began to negotiate the details of their separation.

Later, the trainees, supervisor, and therapist discussed the case. The therapist remarked on how striking it had been to watch Raul listen attentively to me as I said essentially the same words that she had spoken to him only moments before. During my subsequent work with families, I have seen this dynamic emerge repeatedly, indicating, as was described within Chapter Four, that many men listen much more attentively and respectfully to other men than to women. The privilege of respectful listening that we men grant another man is habitually denied to women, even when the woman is one's partner with whom one is attempting to rebuild intimacy after committing a major transgression.

No matter how disturbing, you must recognize that patterns of privilege and discrimination, as currency of power, thread through all of our relationships. Moreover, it is important to recognize that when we practice racism, sexism, and other forms of discrimination, we very rarely do it with conscious intent. In other words, Raul did not say to himself, "I don't have to check this investment idea out with Janice before I spend our money or really even listen to what she has to say about anything because she's a woman," and the judges who didn't recognize our institute's faculty of color did not say to themselves, "I don't have to bother remembering the faces of these dark-skinned people." Instead, we act out what we've learned about the power differences within our society *out of habit,* usually below our threshold of awareness. This chapter seeks to help you replace that lack of awareness with critical consciousness and the change in actions that follows.

Eve and George

The amount of money we control is often our most significant source of power. Money grants access to every commodity and resource, from food and shelter to free time to credible representation in courts of law as well as in the court of public opinion. As the following case illustrates, the power, privilege, and vulnerabilities connected to a multitude of personal characteristics—financial wealth, employment status, gender, race, our willingness to use secrecy, and even the fact of a woman's pregnancy—shape the issues that confront couples today.

George and Eve, both of whom are in their early forties and from English-American families dating back to the colonial period, live in a large stately home in one of the wealthiest areas of New Jersey. Eve is a highly-compensated executive at a Manhattan advertising firm who works long hours at a career she finds invigorating. She recently became pregnant, a development that thrilled both members of the couple. Returning home early from work one day, Eve saw George in their home office, hunched over the computer, presumably hard at work. Creeping silently up behind him, intent upon surprising him with an invitation to an early dinner at their favorite restaurant, Eve discovered that George was composing an email to his twenty-year-old girlfriend. Shocked, infuriated, and grief-stricken, Eve called me to schedule a consultation.

I learned that the couple had resided in Manhattan following their marriage fifteen years earlier. Eve, who had started out as an office assistant and risen steadily through the ranks, now earned more than a million dollars annually as one of the firm's key executives. George, after working in construction for a number of years, had opened a hardware store with one of his closest friends. Opening the store had been George's lifelong dream, but after just short of two years, the business failed—a major loss for him. Afterwards, George had had trouble finding steady work, but he periodically landed odd jobs through connections to friends and neighbors. All this happened approximately eighteen months before our consultation.

To continue, a year ago, Eve and George had moved into their current home—a grand residence in a gated community that included a nine-hole golf course, indoor and outdoor swimming pools, and a state-of-the-art tennis facility. Rick, the CEO of Eve's company, also lived in the same community. Over their years of working together, Rick had become Eve's close friend and mentor. He would regale Eve with stories about the fun the two couples would have being neighbors.

Eve had been ambivalent about whether or not to move. Although she and George loved tennis and found Rick and his wife to be great company, she knew George's friends all lived in Manhattan and Queens, and he had been relying heavily upon their moral support since losing his business. She didn't want him to suffer any more losses if possible.

Surprisingly, after they had talked it over, George's enthusiasm for the new home had sealed the deal. He had argued that a change of scenery would be great for his morale; he'd find pleasure in taking care of their new place. George loved carpentry and landscaping but there hadn't been much call for either, residing as they did at the time in a 33rd-floor co-op apartment. Together, the couple had decided to start a whole new way of life with the move. They had even decided to launch one last attempt to start a family, having been unsuccessful in conceiving up to that time.

Shortly after they moved, however, George became depressed. He spent most of his time moping around the house. Sullen and irritable, George refused to talk about his feelings with Eve. Eve had suggested they see a therapist, but George declined. Then, a few months prior to our consultation, George began working part-time as a facilities manager at the tennis club. He had brightened up considerably, talking about how good it was to be connecting to people again and doing something that felt meaningful. He'd had difficulty keeping in touch with his friends in New York and was now making new friends among the "tennis set," as he called them.

As it turned out, the young woman who had been the intended recipient of his email was the daughter of one of the families within the community. George had met her while working at the club.

When we began to discuss issues of power, George said that he felt less and less "like a man" as Eve began to outpace his level of income, but that he regained his masculinity during the time he owned the hardware store. He had kept these feelings from Eve because "talking about them would have made me feel even worse." He said that he appreciated Eve's steadfast desire to keep all of their funds in joint holdings. George cried as he remembered Eve's motto: "We're a team so everything we have belongs equally to both of us." He said that the more she gave to him the worse he felt about himself, but he wouldn't talk about this with anyone.

George said the affair with the young woman made him feel "more like a man." He went on to describe how, "In some sick way when Eve got pregnant I felt like it made it even more easy for me to act on the opportunity that presented itself—I guess I felt like she was definitely stuck with me now." Notice that George used his secret extramarital affair as a way to counter his feeling of wounded masculinity and increase his power relative to Eve. These choices, along with his unwillingness to ask for help with the emotional pain he was feeling, brought on the relationship crisis.

Keith and Janine

When power and privilege are faced head on, when the male code and male entitlement are critically examined and challenged, partners free themselves to move away from power as domination and toward the power of collaboration and love.

Keith and Janine, both in their late thirties, are an African-American couple with an eighteen-month-old daughter, Cherie. Janine works as a call center director for a major U.S. bank. Keith, who used to be employed as a technology services manager at the corporate headquarters of the same bank that employs Janine, has worked as a stay-at-home dad since Cherie's arrival. Both members of the couple give every indication of their satisfaction with the current arrangement. Janine's income, larger than her husband's, is now being deposited into three accounts—one that covers shared expenses, and the overflow evenly divided in two—one account for Janine and a second for Keith.

There is passion in Janine's voice as she describes her desire to become a financial services executive, an aspiration she seems well on her way toward achieving. Keith, whose father was his family's main caregiver for much of his childhood, feels comfortable in his current role and says he's proud to be taking such good care of Cherie and his family. He has come to see his function as a stay-at-home father as an expansion of the role that men typically lead in the lives of their families, and in no way as undermining his masculinity. "Actually, I was glad to let go of that stuff about being the 'breadwinner' and 'master of my castle.' At first I felt a little like I was less of a man or something like that, but I talked about it a lot with Janine, my father, and my friends. With their support I came around to see that it's a gift to be able to be there with Cherie for all of her firsts. I thank God and Janine every day for this opportunity!"

The couple sees this as a long term arrangement that will, as Cherie enters pre-school and then elementary school, eventually allow Keith more time to pursue his dream of becoming an author. Keith and Janine have negotiated a balance of power that feels equitable to both, and their relationship appears to be flourishing

The power of collaboration and love is attainable, as Keith and Janine's story attests. With courage and the support of a loving network of friends and family, we can shift attitudes of entitlement and resist the dictates of the male code. I challenge you to examine your own most significant relationships, identify where you are participating in power as domination, and work toward change. Later chapters provide you with more ideas on how to go about doing this.

The goal of this chapter is to focus your attention on power as an organizing feature of relationships. While rarely acknowledged, power and its associated privileges are hidden within the blueprints for all relationships, including intimate ones. I described two visions of power, the first associated with domination and the second with love. For a deeper look at the two, I recommend reading Riane Eisler's *The Chalice and the Blade,* which provides a comprehensive and brilliant analysis of the two notions of power, their gendered connections, and their history.

I spent the bulk of the chapter discussing power as domination because that, unfortunately, is the kind of power that overwhelmingly structures life within our society. Exploring case examples, we identified a number of identity aspects and their associated implications for the dynamics of power within relationships. Please keep in mind that almost any identifiable human characteristic adds dimensions to the power equation that shapes an interpersonal relationship.

We are not done exploring power and control. Chapter Six examines what happens when imbalances of power are taken to their extreme.

✦ ✧ ✦ **ACTION STEPS** ✦ ✧ ✦

REFER TO THE LIST OF PERSONAL ATTRIBUTES BELOW FOR THE ACTION STEPS THAT FOLLOW.

- ✧ gender
- ✧ skin color
- ✧ financial resources
- ✧ sexual orientation
- ✧ age
- ✧ state of health or disability
- ✧ educational background

- social class background
- network of family and friends
- profession
- languages we are able to speak
- accent with which we speak English
- skill at articulating thoughts and feelings
- talents we possess
- spirituality
- religion
- secrets we hold
- physical attractiveness
- size and strength

✦ ✧ ✦ ACTION STEPS ✦ ✧ ✦
MEN

1. Have a conversation with a close male friend about how each of the attributes listed above contributes to the power you each hold.

2. Describe for each other at least one time when you took your personal power for granted and/or used it to over-power or disadvantage another person or persons.

3. Brainstorm at least five specific actions you can take that will use your power to increase fairness for others. Examples include:

   - Insisting that your father, brother, or son respect-fully interact with a female family member he treats dismissively.
   - If you are heterosexual, advocating for the rights of gay, lesbian, bisexual, and transgender people within your community of faith or workplace.

⬥ If you have professional status, using your power at business meetings to invite people with less status to contribute.

4. Get together with the same friend two weeks later. Describe for each other how you followed through with the actions you chose and the resulting benefits. Continue to support each other in finding ways to use your power to empower others.

✦ ✧ ✦ ACTION STEPS ✦ ✧ ✦
WOMEN

1. Arrange a conversation with one or more close women friends. Share experiences in which each of you decided against using (or even acknowledging) your power in order to let a man pass as more intelligent, educated, wealthy, strong, physically fit, energetic, attractive, talented, skilled, articulate, witty, funny, cultured, worldly, accomplished, socially prominent, important, or powerful.

2. Identify the pressures that compel women and girls to make these kinds of decisions and the potential consequences for those who assert their power.

3. Describe three actions that each participant in the conversation can take to increase her power, or assert her power. Examples include:

⬥ Signing up for a training/class/degree program.
⬥ Speaking up the next time she disagrees during a family discussion or a meeting at work.

⋄ Standing her ground with her partner when he/she challenges her decision about spending or saving money.

4. Discuss the likely benefits that will result from these actions. Also discuss the negative consequences that may result. Brainstorm how to respond to these negative consequences.

5. Ask each of your friends to commit to following through with at least one action. Schedule a follow-up discussion with the same group of friends and discuss the progress that's been made.

✦ ✧ ✦ **ACTION STEPS** ✦ ✧ ✦
COUPLES

1. Consider the two visions of power identified in this chapter: "power over" and "power with." Identify at least three examples of "power over" from each of your daily lives. Examples may come from your workplaces, extended families, and community organizations. Talk about what it feels like when others exert "power over" you.

2. Identify three examples of "power with" from your couple partnership. These may involve the way you address household finances, division of shared responsibilities, community activities, leisure pursuits, your work lives, or caring for children, pets, and elders.

3. Brainstorm a number of actions that would increase the power you have with each other. An example would be to

take turns watching the children or pets so that each of you has time to take a class, create artwork, enjoy time with friends, or enrich yourself and your partnership in another manner. Another example would be to initiate an activity together—join a health club, enroll in a massage or yoga class, or plan a vacation. A third example would be for each partner to teach the other a new skill, such as how to use a computer application, prepare a favorite food, knit, or practice progressive relaxation.

4. Commit to enacting at least one of the options you've identified.

5. After following through with your plan, talk about how what you've done adds to the experience of love within your partnership.

6

Recognizing Abuse

✦ ✧ ✦

A great deal can be learned about a culture through its time-honored tales, and few "love stories" have reached the prominence of "Beauty and the Beast." Disney's version, which you can see on film, on the Broadway stage, and even on ice, continues to be a fantastic commercial success. Live productions bring audiences to tears and to their feet for ovations around the world. While the songs and staging are undeniably beguiling, a closer look reveals the presence of a sinister theme. The story offers a stunning example of how male violence against women is often taken for granted, even romanticized, in artistic productions. And art, as we've so often heard, reflects life.

If you have access to the film, which is likely for readers who are parents or grandparents, I encourage you to watch it again to refresh your memory. I'm going to describe how Disney's movie version of *Beauty and the Beast* depicts a young woman who is stalked by one man and then held captive and terrorized by a second. In doing so, I do not mean to discredit this film in any way. It is a masterpiece of animation and music. Instead, what I mean to do is show that themes of male entitlement and power as domination are so fundamental to mainstream American culture that they pervade even our most benign cultural stories. This film provides a particularly useful example, but countless others carry the same themes. I'll use the film to illustrate how the traditional male code and male entitlement provide a foundation for abuse.

After discussing segments of the film that exemplify these points, I'll define and further discuss the types of abuse that are common in dating and committed partnerships. I'll provide information about the incidence of abuse, the reasons why it continues to occur, and case examples from real-life situations. The chapter concludes with an examination of common misconceptions about abuse.

BEAUTY AND THE BEAST

Disney's animated film, *Beauty and the Beast*, tells the story of a beautiful young woman named Belle. The people of her village consider Belle odd because, instead of preparing for marriage, housewifery, and child-rearing, she spends hours reading about the world beyond small town life. Gaston, the town's unrivaled paragon of masculinity by virtue of his enormous physical stature, muscularity, handsome face, hunting skills, and unrelenting bravado, wants to marry Belle.

In the film's opening scene, Gaston stalks Belle through their village. Brushing his way past people on the street and climbing over buildings to make haste, he finally jumps from a rooftop and lands directly in front of Belle. When he fails to dazzle her with his small talk, Gaston grabs the book she's holding, tosses it into the mud, and commands Belle to "start paying attention to more important things, like me!"

As Gaston badgers Belle, the townspeople greet one another, sing, and gossip all around the pair. Do the townspeople save Belle from Gaston's unwelcome attention? Do they shout for someone to alert the gendarmes (the story's set in France)? Do they call Gaston an arrogant and insensitive lout, and sing about how somebody needs to set him straight about common decency? Does anybody, male or female, challenge him? Hardly. The townspeople's lyrics in this and later scenes decry Belle as a head-in-the-clouds fool for passing up the attentions of the town's most desirable bachelor. (Keep this in mind, because the unwillingness of community members, particularly men, to hold those who commit abuse responsible allows the problem to flourish.) Belle eventually escapes by smiling sweetly, joking with Gaston, and saying she needs to get home to her father.

Not one who gives up easily, Gaston, unbeknownst to Belle, sets a date for their wedding. When that special day arrives, Gaston's friends assemble decorated tables, a preacher, and a band of musicians waiting for their cue just outside Belle's home. The townspeople gather in anticipation of the big moment. The only thing left to do is inform Belle!

Gaston knocks on her front door and then bursts into her home, not bothering to wait for an invitation. "Today is the day your dreams come true!" he announces. Helping himself to a seat at her table, Gaston leans back and plunks his muddy boots on top of the open pages of Belle's book.

She asks, "What do you know about my dreams, Gaston?"

"Plenty," he replies. He tells her to imagine "a rustic hunting lodge, my latest kill roasting on the fire" and "six or seven" sons—"strapping boys, like me."

Belle casts about for some manner of escape as she backs away from him. Gaston pins her against the wall. She manages to slip under one of his outstretched arms and makes her way toward the front door. He follows, commanding her to marry him after tossing a wooden chair to the floor. He pins her again, this time against the front door. Belle flings the door open as Gaston leans his weight against it, causing him to stumble out. She locks the door behind him.

In this and other scenes from the movie, Gaston's actions epitomize male entitlement, rigid adherence to the male code, and power as domination taken to the furthest extreme. His behavior reveals the connections between male entitlement, the male code, and the tactics of abuse of power at the heart of dating and domestic violence: intimidation, emotional abuse, isolation, using children, using male privilege, coercion, and threats.

For example, Rule #1 ("Don't act like a girl!"), along with Rule #6 ("Be dominant!"), have taught Gaston to value himself more than he values women and to see his wife as property. He's fully convinced of his right to make a number of life-changing decisions for Belle. In fact, Gaston feels entitled to decide every aspect of her future. He's decided whom she'll marry, and when, how she'll spend her time (cooking, cleaning, and taking care of Gaston's sons), and where she'll live. Gaston decides that he'll isolate Belle in a "rustic hunting lodge." One can imagine how completely she'd be cut off from family and friends who live within the town's limits were she living in a lodge off in the woods, isolated, caring for her many sons and husband. Gaston's desire for children lacks any consideration for Belle. He even presumes they'll be boys, marking their main value as their reflection of his "strapping" masculinity.

Gaston follows Rule #2 ("Keep your feelings to yourself!"), as do many men who choose to be abusive, to such an extreme that he seems to have no feelings aside from anger and the drive to control himself and others. Where we'd expect Gaston to show kindness, as when he encounters Belle strolling through the village, instead he bullies her. Rather than inviting Belle into a conversation about how she's doing or admiring her passion for the world of ideas, he throws her book into the mud and scolds her. Where we'd expect Gaston to demonstrate love, he demonstrates domination and control instead.

Rule #4 ("Be self-reliant!") encourages men to trust their own judgment exclusively. Gaston listens to nothing said by the woman he wants to marry, recognizing her refusals only as obstacles to overcome. As with so many perpetrators of abuse, Gaston believes everything would be great if only Belle would come to her senses and follow his orders. Gaston's extreme self-reliance turns Belle into an object to be manipulated rather than a person with thoughts, feelings, and needs of her own.

Gaston's foray into Belle's home in an attempt to gain her hand in marriage shows how Rule #5 ("Be aggressive") promotes violence. Colleagues of mine use this piece of the film with the sound turned off during training sessions. They play the videotape, starting from where Gaston shoves open the front door and ending when Belle sets him up to stumble out of her house, then ask viewers to identify the interaction depicted. People unfamiliar with the film can't believe it when told they have watched a marriage proposal; typically, they guess an attempted robbery or rape. Gaston's posturing, furniture-throwing, and relentless pursuit looks even nastier with the dialogue silenced. Like Gaston, too many men use aggression to try to resolve relationship conflicts. It always makes things worse.

As though Gaston's interaction with Belle isn't scary enough, Belle later gets captured by an enormous and horrifying beast, who subjects her to all sorts of intimidation, threats, and loud abusive tirades. Because the Beast alternates between abusive outbursts and displays of vulnerability and gallantry, Belle begins to develop warm feelings for her captor. (It is important to note that most perpetrators of abuse behave this way—they do not always act like monsters.) Belle's warm feelings for the Beast come not a moment too soon, for his time is running out. Let me explain. The Beast was once a human being, a handsome prince, in fact. He got into trouble several years back by insulting a woman who stopped by his castle seeking shelter from a storm. Less forgiving than Belle (perhaps because she held much more power), this woman, who turned out to be a witch, cursed the prince into his current beastly form. She sentenced him to die if he couldn't make a woman fall in love with him by a date now fast approaching. Just in the nick of time, Belle announces her love for the Beast, thus saving his life. The curse lifts, he morphs into a handsome young prince, and the couple—you guessed it—lives happily ever after.

This story teaches that a good and loving woman, acting all by herself, can save a man from himself; she can transform an abusive beast into the loving man he was meant to be. We also learn that an overly powerful and unforgiving witch—today, perhaps read "bitch"—can turn a prince into a beast. *Whichever way it goes, a woman is responsible for the man's change.*

Beauty and the Beast teaches boys to believe that the right girl or woman will provide infinite tolerance and understanding. She will teach him how to love. The tale teaches girls to hang in there when they're being disrespected or even abused because a woman's job is to civilize the man she loves.

The next time you show this film to your children or grandchildren, talk with them about these messages. You may be thinking, "I'll just try to avoid exposing them to stories that include these kinds of messages." Good luck with that, because these messages are everywhere. We can't avoid them. We can develop critical consciousness, however. And that's what you'll be helping young people do through conversations that identify and explore these themes.

DEFINING ABUSE

Before exploring real-life case examples, I think it helps to define abuse more comprehensively. The term, often used interchangeably with domestic or dating violence, identifies a systematic misuse of power in which one partner uses a number of tactics to dominate and control the other partner. While the recipient of abusive behavior is most frequently the partner whom the abusive individual seeks to dominate, others who are close to the victimized partner frequently become targets, also. These may include her children, parents, siblings, friends, and coworkers. Likewise, pets are frequent targets of assault. All of the abusive partner's tactics are directed toward controlling, coercing, or limiting the options open to the victimized partner.

While the abusive tactics that come most readily to mind may fall under the category of physical assault, this is only one amid the broad collection of tactics that most abusive individuals employ. Indeed, some abusive relationships never involve physical assault, yet the impact can be just as horrific as those that do. It is quite common for people who have experienced abusive relationships to state that the emotionally abusive aspect of the partner's repertoire was far more wounding than the physical beatings.

A number of abusive tactics were mentioned earlier in this chapter. The following list expands upon these and provides examples. Please note that the pronoun "she" is used to designate the victim of abuse because the overwhelming majority of abuse within relationships is perpetrated by men against women. I do not, however, mean to imply that men are never the victims of domestic violence. There are also instances of women abusing men, men abusing men, and women abusing women. The list that follows also appears in Appendix A at the end of the book in the form of a handout useful for helping people identify abuses of power within their intimate relationships.

ABUSES OF POWER
WITHIN INTIMATE RELATIONSHIPS:

✦ **Using male privilege:** Treating her like a servant. Insisting on making all the "big" decisions. Acting like the "master of the castle." Neglecting second shift responsibilities such as parenting, laundry, grocery shopping, housework, coordinating the children's school-related and recreational activities, elder care, and family medical care.

✦ **Isolation:** Controlling what she does, who she sees and talks to, where she goes. Denying access to transportation. Removal of support system by relocation to a new residence.

✦ **Emotional abuse:** Putting her down or making her feel bad about herself. Calling her names. Trying to make her think she's crazy. Playing mind games. Stonewalling.

✦ **Intimidation:** Putting her in fear by using looks, actions, gestures, and loud voices. Smashing things, destroying property. Driving car at excessive speed.

✦ **Stalking:** Persistent pursuit and unwanted attention that can include in-person following, visits, and pursuit using phone, email, mail, and unwanted gifts.

✦ **Economic abuse:** Trying to keep her from getting or keeping a job. Controlling her knowledge of assets and/or access to money. Hiding assets.

✦ **Using immigration status:** Use of her undocumented status to threaten her with deportation or loss of job, children, or medical care.

✦ **Using children:** Making her feel guilty about the

children. Using the children to give her messages. Using visitation with the children as an opportunity to harass her. Irresponsible parenting. Abusive and controlling behavior toward the children.

+ **Threats:** Threatening to do something to hurt her or someone she loves emotionally or physically. Threatening to commit suicide, report her to welfare, take away the children and/or her emotional support system, or disrupt her workplace. In gay or lesbian relationships, threatening to "out" one's partner to their workplace, friends, or family.

+ **Seduction:** Gifts, extravagant shows of remorse, and promises of change without any follow-through: i.e. doesn't take full responsibility for the abusiveness by enrolling in a batterer's treatment program and following through completely, doesn't endorse a period of separation whose time frame is determined by his partner, doesn't offer to leave the couple's residence while ensuring financial support of his partner as necessary (and children if applicable).

+ **Sexual abuse:** Making her do sexual things against her will. Physically attacking the sexual parts of her body. Criticizing her sexual performance. Indulging in outside sexual encounters. Exposing her to HIV by not practicing safer sex. Insisting on sexual contact after assaulting her. Repeatedly pursuing her for sex.

+ **Physical abuse:** Slapping, pinching, pushing, shoving, punching, choking, biting, entrapment, beating, kicking, grabbing, pulling hair, stabbing, shooting, killing.

PREVALENCE OF DOMESTIC
AND DATING VIOLENCE

It is important to note that in more than 90% of heterosexual relationships where there is domestic or dating violence, the man is the perpetrator. It is also important to note that domestic and dating violence occur with similar frequency across all dimensions of diversity, including social class, ethnicity, religious background, skin color, sexual orientation, professional status, and educational background. As provided by the National Domestic Violence Hotline, the following statistics indicate that domestic violence and abuse within dating relationships are very common:

+ 31% of American women report being physically or sexually abused by a husband or boyfriend at some point in their lives.

+ 503,485 women are stalked by an intimate partner each year in the United States.

+ Approximately 4 million women in America are physically abused by their husbands or live-in partners each year.

+ In 2000, 33.5 % of all female murder victims in the U.S. were killed by their intimate partners (latest statistic available).

+ 40% of girls age 14-17 know someone their age who has been hit or beaten by a boyfriend.

+ One in five female high school students reports being physically or sexually abused by a dating partner.

+ Family violence within the U.S. costs from $5-10 billion annually in medical expenses.

+ Husbands and boyfriends commit 13,000 acts of violence against women in the workplace every year.

WHY DOES HE DO IT?

This is an important question to ask because it lays responsibility for violence squarely on the shoulders of those who perpetrate it. (There has been far too much attention given the victim-blaming question, "Why does she stay?") Because the power of domination guides most human interactions, rather than the power of love and collaboration, the stage is always set for abuse to occur. Domestic and dating violence are the most extreme expressions of power as domination within intimate connections. The male code exacerbates the likelihood of abuse by teaching men to feel entitled to deference from women and by equipping them poorly to deal with their emotions in ways other than the expression of anger. Finally, there are often rapid turnaround rewards and no consequences for those who choose to be abusive. More specifically, many men choose to be abusive because:

+ *they can*—Whether because of body size and strength, control of weapons, connections to others, financial resources, or some other source of power, the person who chooses to be abusive holds power over the one being abused.
+ *it works*—The tactics of abuse are usually effective, at least in the short term, in getting the abused to do what the abuser wants them to do.
+ *nobody stops them*—Abuse relies upon a lack of community interference, which functions as tacit support for the perpetuation of abuse. Our society continues to value an individual or couple's privacy over most everything else, including the safety of women and children.

CASE EXAMPLES

Dominic and Lucy

In the first couple relationship described below, a husband initiates a number of abusive tactics after a change in the power balance within his marriage. In subsequent case examples, we'll examine relationships in which the severity of abuse is even more advanced.

Dominic and Lucy are a white couple in their mid-thirties. Dominic, who comes from a mostly Italian-American family, makes his living selling furniture to restaurants and other businesses. Gregarious and opinionated, Dominic makes an immediate impression upon his customers and does well at his profession. Lucy, whose family background is Irish and German, had worked at home taking care of the couple's two children, now aged ten and six, until three years ago, when she began her current job as an administrative assistant at a small insurance agency. She enjoys her work and is well-liked by her employer and coworkers. While Lucy earns only half of what Dominic does, she's nonetheless thrilled to have this income and feels great about contributing to the work of the team at her agency.

Initially, Dominic had seemed pleased with Lucy's return to the world of work. He had complimented her on her initiative and encouraged her confidence. Another response was growing, though. Dominic noticed that Lucy was paying less attention to the housework and the children's needs, including supervision of their homework, arranging play dates, getting them to their sporting events, and other aspects of their schedule. He made comments to Lucy that he felt she was "letting the family slide."

In the past, when Dominic had criticized Lucy, she had always been contrite; now, she was furious. Before Lucy's return to paid employment, she had taken care of all the details of family life and home management, which had seemed to include all her waking hours nearly every day. After she started working at the agency, she quickly recognized that "nine to five" was easier than her previous work hours. She told Dominic in no uncertain terms that she wasn't going to work full-time and then come home and do all the housework and childcare while he felt no inclination to share these responsibilities. She began placing demands upon Dominic to pull his fair share of weight on the second shift.

Dominic reacted to Lucy's increased assertiveness and demands for more equal distribution of family labor as though they were a withdrawal of love. Rather than consider the merits of her argument, he labeled Lucy's complaints "bitching."

"I used to think she loved me, but now her true colors are coming out—I guess I was mostly just a meal ticket." Dominic began to imagine that Lucy was being unfaithful to him.

Things went rapidly downhill. Always somewhat jealous, Dominic now began paying an inordinate amount of attention to Lucy's schedule and whereabouts. Whenever she took longer than he thought an errand or her drive home ought to take, Dominic would interrogate her: "No way it could've taken you that long. Where were you really?!!"

Outraged, Lucy would shout back to Dominic that he'd "better stop giving her the third degree!"

Thinking that if he confronted her while the children were home she was less likely to challenge him, Dominic began to issue his investigative tirades in more quiet tones, and almost exclusively when the children were present. Lucy was at a loss to understand this behavior. She began feeling depressed and increasingly irritable.

Eventually convincing himself that Lucy was having an affair, Dominic began secretly monitoring her email. He found a note she had addressed to one of her male friends complaining that "Dominic is trying to control my every move—I'm at the breaking point." When Dominic confronted her with this as evidence of infidelity, Lucy decided he was losing his mind.

Dominic and Lucy's problems, as well as their potential solutions, begin to come into focus only when we look at their interaction against the backdrop of the traditional male code, power as domination, and tactics of abuse. During the early years of their marriage, Dominic and Lucy had a relationship that was in alignment with the traditional male code. Lucy's re-entry into the workplace changed this status quo.

Neither Lucy nor Dominic thinks about the dynamics of power, male entitlement, or the rules of the male code as they try to make sense of what is happening in their relationship. Applying the tools they have—ideas about love, communication, and mental illness—only increase their feelings of confusion and despair.

With the validation, monetary income, and experience of expanding competence that Lucy gains at her workplace, there's a growing recognition of the inequities within her relationship with Dominic. For example, it becomes clear to Lucy that at the end of her workday, when there is still much to do at home, Dominic not only expects her to do it all, but he enforces this expectation by supervising her.

Dominic can't believe that his lack of equal involvement with the housework and childcare strikes Lucy as a problem. Like many heterosexual men, he believes that his wife should provide these services. This belief is supported by the fact that Lucy had never challenged these expectations in the past. Moreover, Rules #1 ("Don't act like a girl!"), #3 ("Work is your first priority!"), and #7 ("Be dominant!"), had long assured Dominic that his role was to bring home the bacon and then sit back and rule over his domicile. In other words, Dominic had been thoroughly convinced of his entitlement to male privilege. When Lucy asked that he contribute more to the work of maintaining a home and family, he experienced it as an assault on his masculinity—a challenge to his power and entitlement as "man of the house."

In keeping with Rule #2 ("Keep your feelings to yourself!"), Dominic doesn't identify and thoughtfully process the range of feelings—i.e. confusion, sadness, and grief—that were probably brewing in response to Lucy's demands. Instead, he reacts defensively, angrily concluding that Lucy is a bitch who sees him only as a meal ticket. In keeping with Rule #4 ("Be self-reliant!"), he doesn't talk about what is going on with loving friends and family members, but keeps the matter to himself. The result is that, rather than critically examining his privilege, power, and entitlement, Dominic enacts them through an escalating pattern of abusive tactics.

Applying Rule #5 ("Be aggressive!"), he berates Lucy for "letting the family slide," using the children's presence as a way to elevate his control over her during these verbal assaults. (Remember, Dominic had observed that Lucy was less likely to scream back at him if the children were at home) Dominic also tries to isolate Lucy from sources of support by monitoring and complaining about her time away from the family. He justifies this behavior by convincing himself that Lucy was having an affair—thereby concocting a way to blame her for *his* coercive and emotionally abusive actions.

Lucy sees that Dominic's unreasonable demands upon her create their relationship crisis—demands that she do almost all of the childcare and housework, make her whereabouts known to him at all times, tolerate unrelenting inquisitions about her travel time, and maintain only those social contacts that meet his approval. She does not recognize Dominic's demands as escalating attempts to restore the power imbalance that had existed before she assumed paid employment; instead, she sees his actions as evidence of his laziness, jealousy, "hot temper," and, finally, mental illness.

Systematic abuse of power within relationships is rarely identified as such because most people, like Lucy and Dominic, do
not evaluate the power dynamics within their partnership as a
possible source of their difficulties. In fact, most women, by
virtue of their gender socialization, are likely to search far and
wide within themselves when trying to figure out what's going
wrong in their relationship, holding themselves accountable first
and foremost. Men, by the way, are likely to do the same—hold
their woman partners accountable for relationship problems—
because they too have been taught to assign most relationship
responsibilities to women and not to themselves.

When most people evaluate their relationship, they start by
looking for things like differences of opinion, misunderstandings,
communication difficulties, problematic personality traits, and,
after all other options are exhausted, signs of mental illness. The
questions that actually help Dominic and Lucy acknowledge
what's going on in their relationship and decide what to do next
have little to do with *these* issues. Instead, the following types of
questions, which explore the male code, entitlement, power, and
privilege, help them begin to get a handle on their conflict:

+ How much time does each of you devote to housework, childcare, and social planning activities? Are
  you willing to keep a log for a week to find out?
+ How would you say the amount of time you spend
  on these activities has changed since Lucy starting
  working outside of the home?
+ Now that you have a baseline and some history to
  work from, what do you see as being an equitable
  distribution of these household and family responsibilities as you move into the future?

+ If your answer to this question is not "we should both do an equal share," what are your reasons for thinking otherwise?

+ If it is uncomfortable to imagine taking on a more equal share of household responsibilities, why is that? What would it mean to you about yourself if you were to do so?

+ What ideas about yourself as a man or woman are being challenged by the difficulties the two of you have been experiencing recently?

+ What ideas about yourself as a man or woman would be challenged by creating a more equal distribution of household and family responsibilities?

+ What do you think it was about Lucy's assumption of paid employment that contributed to the shift in the balance of household and family responsibilities?

+ How did Lucy's new job change the balance of power between the two of you?

+ In what ways do you think this change increased and decreased the kinds and amounts of power you each hold?

+ In what ways have you tried to restore the old balance of power and/or maintain the new one?

These questions help the couple move toward developing critical consciousness. They bring issues of power, privilege, and entitlement out of the shadows so that these profoundly relevant realities can be dealt with directly. With these questions I help Dominic and Lucy shape a more useful understanding of what's going on and how to make things better.

Miriam and Richard

Even when abusive tactics become far more extreme than those of Dominic and Lucy, the situation is frequently defined by the participants, along with those around them, as something other than abuse. Miriam is a fifty-seven-year-old Russian-Jewish-American woman who has been married for thirty-seven years to Richard, also fifty-seven years old and from the same ethnic and religious background. Miriam works as a medical assistant and Richard is a very successful jewelry salesman. For as long as she can remember, Miriam has tried to work around Richard's temper. Richard yells, screams, and pounds his fist on counters and tables—twice even put his fist through sheetrock walls—when things aren't to his liking.

"He has to be right about absolutely everything or he starts screaming and yelling. It's just not worth it to do anything that might get him started. He's been on this kick for the past month now where he wants me to go to temple with him every week. I don't know where this sudden love for his faith came from—he never attended all that much in the past. I really don't feel like going. I've just been going with him these past few weeks because it's not worth the nonsense he'd put me through if I refused." Miriam goes on to explain that Richard "has never hit me or anybody else in the family, and I'm really not scared of him, but he's been so loud for so long that I actually think he's damaged my hearing."

The couple has two young adult sons: Jacob, twenty-six, lives with his wife in a nearby town, and Rob, twenty-one, lives with his parents. Miriam consulted me because Richard "has been all over Rob, recently."

"Rob works part time at a camera store and goes to college full-time. Richard's always yelling at him that he needs to get a better job and stop putting so much stock in his schooling, which

Richard considers a waste of time. Rob came to me in a rage and fighting back tears the other evening, saying he thinks he's gonna 'punch Dad out' if he doesn't get off his back. I don't know what to do anymore!"

I asked Miriam to look at the power and control wheel, a reference sheet identifying the tactics of abuse listed within the previous section of this chapter. She studied it for several minutes, sat back with a sigh, and said, "Richard does all of these things except stalking and the physical and sexual abuse. The stuff about immigration doesn't apply to us. I never considered any of these to be abuse, though, just normal everyday life."

This is a common story and it doesn't mean that Miriam is unperceptive or weak. Instead, this story emphasizes the way that everybody around Richard and Miriam, including his parents and siblings, coaches, schoolteachers, friends, and coworkers, has normalized his lifelong pattern of loud, demanding, and abusive behavior.

Richard's extreme and rigid adherence to rules #5 ("Be aggressive!"), and #6 ("Be dominant!") are evidenced by the description above. Discussions with Richard and his son, Rob, provided more evidence of how rigid adherence to the traditional male code was central to Richard's abusiveness toward Miriam, as to well as the growing conflict between father and son.

There's a point I'd like to make before moving on to another example. As you read this case description, you may have found yourself thinking, "Yes, Richard's been communicating his concerns in all the wrong ways, but I wonder why he's on this kick about temple and also putting so much pressure on his son to do better economically—could it be that he's worried about something, maybe some physical symptoms are scaring him into awareness of his own mortality, for example, and he doesn't know how to talk about that?"

My answer to that question is, "Maybe, but that's not the first thing to pay attention to here. This guy needs to stop being abusive right away!"

It is typical within our society to try to empathize with the reasons for someone's behavior, particularly a white heterosexual man's behavior, before seriously focusing on the impact of his behavior upon others. Another way to say this is that individuals like Richard are typically given every manner of support except support that also comes with accountability—and that's the only kind that's likely to help Richard stop hurting the people he says he loves. Yes, it will be important to help Richard identify his own fears and pains, but *only after he's stopped hurting others and takes responsibility for his abusiveness.* The best way to accomplish that is through Richard's participation in a group process with other men who are working to understand and challenge the traditional male norms and the patterns of abuse associated with them. With men like Richard, individual therapy and any kind of couples therapy are likely to exacerbate the problem.

Anoop and Alice

The community surrounding a domestic violence situation, including work organizations, often support the violence. Alice, a forty-three-year-old Swiss-American mother of two young adult sons, and Anoop, a fifty-year-old Southeast Asian-American father who also has two young adult sons, were married approximately one year ago. Their marriage followed an eight year period during which the couple lived together in Alice's home whenever Anoop was in the United States. Both partners' first marriages ended in divorce approximately fifteen years earlier.

Anoop works as a senior executive at a major US corporation and earns more than five million dollars annually. Upon their marriage, he asked Alice to quit her work as a full professor at one of America's foremost academic institutions in order to be his full-time career helpmate. She agreed, thus embarking upon a new career that centered on entertaining Anoop's business contacts at an endless parade of social commitments, company dinners, and charitable events. "My job was to be charming and fun—to help cement Anoop's connection to the company's CEO, his wife, and everybody else Anoop was in business with," said Alice. At her new "job," Alice became friendly with a number of the corporation's most senior executives and their wives.

Behind what appeared in public to be a loving relationship was an escalating pattern of abuse. While Anoop had always demonstrated jealousy regarding Alice's relationships with her friends, both men and women, this pattern became far more pronounced following the couple's marriage. Anoop mounted a campaign to isolate Alice. In addition to his request that she interrupt her career, Anoop insisted that the couple relocate from the city where Alice had lived for many years to a new home in a city closer to his company's U.S. headquarters. Following the move, Anoop rebuffed Alice, who was now disconnected from her previous social network, whenever she sought to become involved with volunteer or other activities not related to his company. He ridiculed these attempts to establish new connections as "senseless time wasting activities." Anoop protested Alice's phone calls to her friends and family members, none of whom lived locally. His new refrain was, "Isn't your husband enough company for you?" Anoop also stalked Alice by phone. He frequently traveled to the Far East on business. During such trips he called Alice multiple times daily and often throughout the night as well, depending upon his location, "just to make sure she was okay." He even tried to limit her involvement with her sons, complaining that when they visited during college vacations she forgot all about him. He told her that they treated him in a manner that was "ungrateful."

As you can see, wrapped into these tactics of isolation was a great deal of emotional abuse. Alice noted that Anoop never just said what was on his mind in a simple manner. Instead, he gave her a lecture—more of a tirade, actually—and these sometimes went on for several hours. For example, he would shout a proclamation about how ungrateful the boys were, and, from this opening volley, he'd pour out a lecture that she'd be expected to listen to for as long as he felt necessary. She said, "I'm not sure why I'd listen; I guess he started these many years ago and I just learned that if I waited it out, the lecture would be shorter than if I tried to argue with him. Also, he had me convinced that if I tried to interrupt or cut the lecture short this showed some kind of gross disrespect on my part."

On the evening before he and Alice were scheduled to make the long drive to their new home several states away from the apartment Alice had just relinquished, Anoop produced a prenuptial agreement. He informed Alice that this was merely a formality and asked her to sign. This confused Alice because she had already signed one prenuptial agreement several days previously. Anoop explained that his lawyer said some minor changes were necessary and, therefore, the document needed to be revised and signed again. Surprised, exhausted from the preparation to move, and unsettled by the fact that Anoop had not mentioned this issue previously but now seemed to be presenting it with some degree of urgency, Alice said she needed time to consider the new document. Enraged, Anoop began shouting at Alice that she didn't trust him and that she had better sign the document to prove her love.

When Alice argued that it was reasonable for her to read the document carefully before signing, Anoop grabbed her by both wrists, yanked her up from her chair, and pushed her backward away from the table. For several days thereafter, bruises were visible on both of Alice's forearms. Anoop apologized for his behavior, but also commented that Alice bruised too easily. This was the first and only incident of physical abuse Alice experienced. The prenuptial agreements had been substantively changed, granting Alice a greatly decreased settlement in the event of Anoop's death or the couple's divorce. She eventually signed the document.

Anoop used finances as a tactic of abuse and control. Almost as soon as Alice resigned her professorship, Anoop began complaining that she was spending "his money" recklessly. When her sons visited, he complained about how much the food they ate cost. Anoop routinely complained about household expenses, despite the fact that many of the items he complained about were extravagances he alone wanted to buy. It is important to remember that Anoop was making millions of dollars and spending lavishly on all sorts of luxuries, including such things as massages, spa treatments, and dinners at the finest restaurants.

Anoop's exercise of male privilege was pervasive. He insisted on making decisions about almost every aspect of the couple's shared life, including which town they would reside in, which furniture they would purchase, which hotel rooms they would stay in (he always had specific preferences), and when and how they would make love. If Alice disagreed, she was subjected to a harangue. As time went on, the content of Anoop's tirades became more derisive ("You're stupid, vulgar, and disrespectful!") and the tone more threatening.

Anoop's abusiveness provoked a defining crisis in the relationship when he and Alice were in Bermuda attending a business conference that included the company's entire executive leadership team. One morning Alice ventured out with several other company spouses and partners for a guided walking tour of the resort. She did this despite Anoop's instructions for her to remain in their hotel room until he summoned her for the midday business luncheon. When Anoop made an unplanned visit to their room during a break in meetings and found that Alice wasn't there, he canceled his attendance at the balance of the morning's schedule and waited for her return. When she opened the door to their room, Anoop, startling Alice with his presence, seized her by both wrists, pushed her to a seated position on the bed and launched into a furious rant.

"You've disrespected me once again and for the very last time! I told you to stay here in case I needed you and you abandoned that responsibility! You've proven once again that I cannot trust you!" Shaking with rage, he seemed to be struggling to restrain himself from lashing out at her with his hands. He continued, "You're trying to ruin me, aren't you, you conniving bitch! I can't believe that you would do this to me! Haven't I got enough to be concerned about here today? We'll deal with this later because we both have to be at that luncheon in one hour and I've got to talk with Ransom [the CEO] before then, so I have to go!"

Crying and shaking, Alice heard Anoop open and then close the door behind him. After what seemed like several minutes, Alice was finally stirred by a knock at the door. She washed her face quickly in the bathroom, tried to compose herself, and then opened the door to greet Gillian Mantrose, president of the company's largest division and a person Alice considered a friend.

"Glad to find you here, Alice. Are you ready for lunch?" Then, as Gillian noticed how red and shaky Alice looked, she became concerned. "What's going on? Did you just get some bad news? What happened?" she sputtered in her typical rapid-fire staccato.

Alice began sobbing again as she told Gillian what had just occurred, along with some of the details of Anoop's history of abusive and controlling behavior. "I'm really afraid of him at this point—I just want to get out of here and go back home," Alice confided.

"Call security," Gillian offered, as she wrapped one arm around Alice's shoulder, "They'll help you get some space and figure out what to do."

Gillian confided to Alice that she had been in an abusive marriage and knew how confusing and difficult it could be. Together, they called the hotel's security and informed them of the need for an additional room, stressing the need for confidentiality so that Alice would not be found or disturbed. Gillian apologized, explaining that she needed to leave so she could make the luncheon. She asked Alice to phone her later in the afternoon and left. Alice gathered her belongings, packed her bags, and made her way to her new room.

Alice was barely settled in when there was a knock at the door. Keeping the chain hitched, she cracked the door to find Anoop, glaring and stamping in place like a bull about to charge.

"Leave me alone, I need some time and space to think," Alice said softly.

"You have to come back to our room," Anoop ordered, adding, "I can see you are trying to destroy me."

"No," said Alice.

Anoop began leaning against the door with all his weight while trying to cram his hand forward in a vain attempt to unhitch the chain.

"Stop it or I'll call security," Alice warned.

"How do you think I found where you were?" Anoop sneered, "I had Dave [the company's head of security] call the hotel's staff."

"Fine, I'm calling the number for the local police," Alice said, grabbing the nearby phone.

"You'll regret this!" shouted Anoop, shaking his finger at her. He spun around and headed down the corridor.

Alice phoned another senior executive, Pete Jasser, whom she considered a friend. Pete and his wife, Becky, came to her room almost immediately. They arranged for a flight to be booked home within the next two hours. Pete and Becky escorted Alice to the lobby for her taxi. Anoop had either learned that Alice was leaving or was coincidentally in the lobby. He approached, planted himself in front of her so his nose was almost touching hers and launched into a vitriolic stream of insults so vile that Pete felt a need to nudge Anoop aside, place his arm protectively around Alice's shoulder, and escort her to her waiting airport taxi.

During her flight home, Alice made the decision to leave Anoop for good. Having experienced significant support from her social network at Anoop's corporation, she felt validated and empowered. Alice went on to gain crucial support from her friends, parents, two older sisters, a therapist who was knowledgeable about abusive relationships, and a women's support group offered by her county's battered women's shelter.

She was not prepared, however, for what followed. Anoop is a major figure at his company, a "rainmaker." Despite the fact that a number of people were eyewitnesses to his displays of aggression and the aftermath thereof, ranks quickly closed in support of Anoop. Gillian, for example, has never since phoned or returned a phone call from Alice. The same goes for all of Alice's other "friends" at Anoop's company, including Pete and Becky. In fact, the only contact Alice received was unsolicited and from another of the company's executives, John Stowe, who phoned Alice repeatedly encouraging her to reconsider her decision to separate from Anoop.

"He was under stress at the conference and you're causing him so much stress now—I'm worried about his blood pressure; can't you find a way to forgive him and move beyond this?" implored John.

When Alice asked John to consider the stress of living with an abusive partner and encouraged him to refer Anoop to a batterer's intervention program, John said he couldn't imagine that Anoop's behavior "rose to the level of abuse." This kind of institutional and community collusion with perpetrators of abuse is sadly more the rule than the exception.

The path that would have been most responsible and helpful to both Alice and Anoop would have been an attempt to hold Anoop accountable for making changes in his behavior. This could likely have been accomplished by the company's CEO. Had this man advised Anoop that his employment depended upon participation in a men's group that addressed his abusive patterns of behavior, it is likely that Anoop would have complied. Offering support that includes a demand for accountability is the only way to help perpetrators of abuse take their first steps toward change. Too often though, those who have the power to make this happen decline to act. In making this choice, they squander what may be a once-in-a-lifetime opportunity to help the perpetrator of abuse, his partner, and their children.

ABUSE IS *NOT* . . .

It is important to examine some widely held misconceptions about domestic and dating violence. Abusive behavior within a relationship can't be reduced to a personality conflict, "temper," mental health, or substance abuse problem. All of these may have something to do with the particular manner and intensity with which the abuse is carried out, but the abusive pattern itself stems from an attitude of entitlement and from the willingness to enforce that entitlement using violence. In this final section of the chapter we'll look into some of the misconceptions about domestic and dating violence in more detail. These include the myths that abuse is:

+ An "anger management" or temper problem
+ A mental health problem
+ Caused by substance abuse
+ The result of "loving too much"

IT'S NOT ABOUT ANGER

Domestic violence is not caused by insufficient control of one's anger or a "hot temper." Researchers Edward Gondolf and David Russell dispelled this myth in 1986, yet popular understanding continues to lag far behind. "Anger management" approaches presume that anger, or temper, is the problem that needs to be addressed. These approaches offer group education and discussion directed toward helping participants identify situations in which they are likely to become angry, along with strategies for averting angry responses. Participants in anger management programs are taught to do things like count to ten, go for a walk, and do some deep breathing when they feel themselves getting angry at their partner.

The trouble with this approach is that difficulty in controlling anger isn't the problem; the problem is the man's belief in his right to control his partner. If this is still unclear to you, consider the cases described in this chapter. All of the perpetrators of abuse described in the previous examples directed their violence toward their partner. In an upcoming example, the perpetrator directed violence toward those whom he saw as contributing to his loss of control of his partner, including her family members and a police officer. This kind of clearly targeted rage and violence is typical of domestic and dating violence situations. In none of these cases was the abusive partner known to show explosive angry outbursts toward others indiscriminately—for example, at work, on the street, or in other public places like restaurants and stores. The angry outbursts, whether they included physical violence or other forms of abuse, were consistently targeted at the victim.

The perpetrator, therefore, is not "losing control" of his anger. Instead, he is using his anger as a tactic. Here's another fact that helps drive home the point. There are men who "go into rages" and destroy property. No matter how "out of control" such rages may appear to be, it is interesting to observe that, almost unfailingly, the property that ends up getting destroyed or damaged is never property of value to him, but rather property of value to his partner, the victim. If such behavioral incidents were truly the result of loss of control, the damage would be indiscriminate.

Gondolf and Russell note that an unfortunate result of anger management training is that it often makes abusive partners into "even better terrorists." Teaching participants to move away from open expressions of anger seems to sharpen their skills at delivering even more effective tactics in such areas as verbal, emotional, and economic abuse. Another problem with anger management approaches is that, consistent with Rule #2 of the male code ("Keep your feelings to yourself!"), they teach men to even more closely control their feelings. This pushes them farther away from, rather than closer to, self-understanding and empathy toward others.

ABUSIVE BEHAVIOR IS NOT CAUSED BY MENTAL HEALTH OR SUBSTANCE ABUSE PROBLEMS

A friend of mine recently told me about a young couple, Charlie and Nancy, who lived next door to his family for several years. He said, "Every few weeks the neighborhood woke up to Charlie, out of his mind drunk, trying to beat down the front door of his house. Sometimes, the police were called . . . sometimes one or more of the men on the block would go out and calm Charlie down, maybe let him sleep it off at their house or take him to a diner for some coffee."

I asked the friend if Charlie ever went to jail or a batterers' treatment program, and if the couple ever broke up.

With eyes downcast, he said, "I don't think anybody thought much about it . . . the whole neighborhood figured that Charlie just drank a little too much now and then."

"What happened?" I asked, "It sounds like there's more to the story."

My friend continued, "Well, one night he shot Nancy and then himself—they're both dead now—and it turns out he was beating her and controlling her in all kinds of sick ways for years. He wasn't even drinking the day it happened."

Domestic and dating violence are not caused by mental health afflictions or substance abuse. There is great confusion on this point from people of all walks of life, including mental health professionals, substance abuse counseling professionals, police officers, and judges. Men who are arrested for partner abuse frequently make use of this confusion by successfully petitioning courts to allow them to see a psychiatrist or a therapist, or attend AA or other 12-step programs in order to resolve their propensity for committing acts of violence against their partners.

The truth of the matter is that even while an individual struggles with the gravest symptoms of clinical depression, an anxiety disorder, or other mental illness, it is still entirely reasonable to expect that person to behave with civility toward others. The only exception I would include involves people who are struggling with schizophrenia or one of the other psychotic disorders. In such cases, where people are not in touch with consensual reality because they are experiencing hallucinations, delusions, and profoundly disorganized thinking, their behavior can be profoundly disorganized, and this may sometimes include uncivil actions. The patterned, predictable, highly-focused, and goal-directed abuse exhibited by individuals who perpetrate domestic and dating violence is not explainable, however, by mental health diagnoses, and it is not resolved by conventional mental health treatment.

Similarly, alcohol and substance abuse problems do not account for abusive behavior. Many perpetrators of abuse have never had alcohol or substance abuse problems. Conversely, many abusive individuals are well into their alcohol and/or substance abuse recovery. A significant blind spot in 12-step recovery programs (such as Alcoholics Anonymous and Narcotics Anonymous) is made evident by this fact. With their emphasis on the individual's experience of recovery, 12-step communities usually neglect to identify (and, to date, offer no coherent strategy for assisting) recovering individuals who are either perpetrating or on the receiving end of dating and domestic violence.

I'd like to provide one important clarification. There is a relationship between some mental health problems, as well as alcohol and substance abuse, and the perpetration of domestic and dating violence, but the relationship is not causal. In cases where individuals choose to be abusive to their partners and suffer mental health, alcohol, and/or substance abuse problems, the patterns of their abuse are likely to be affected by these problems. For example, if an abusive individual's depression is characterized largely by a flat, depleted mood and lessened energy levels, they are less likely to be abusive when in a depressive episode. However, if their depression is most often characterized by irritability and agitation, then they are likely to be even more dangerous during an acute phase of illness.

Similarly, alcohol and substance abusers are likely to be more or less dangerous while using depending upon the specific impact of their drug of choice. For example, heroin users who are abusive to their partners are apt to be less dangerous while intoxicated due to the subduing affects of the drug, but more dangerous as they enter the discomfort of opiate withdrawal. Alcohol abusers are likely to be more dangerous during the stage of intoxication when inhibitions are decreased but energy levels are not significantly diminished, and less dangerous if they drink to the point where their thinking and behavior are slowed down. In none of these cases, however, will resolving the mental health or substance abuse problem automatically end the abusive behavior. That requires a reshaping of the perpetrator's understanding of his roles and responsibilities as an intimate partner.

ABUSE HAS NOTHING TO DO WITH LOVING TOO MUCH

As the following example shows, it is amazing the degree of denial and blame some people exert in an effort to avoid directly acknowledging and holding men accountable for abusive behavior. A nineteen-year-old Polish-American man from a working class neighborhood in New Jersey refused to accept the fact that his girlfriend no longer wanted to date him. He had been emotionally and physically abusive toward her, and she had wisely decided to end the relationship. The young man walked into her home and stabbed her repeatedly in the face, causing severe but non-lethal lacerations. He then proceeded to light her family's house afire. After exiting the home, he accosted a police officer who had just arrived on the scene. The young man stabbed the police officer several times in his hand, and then stabbed himself in the abdomen.

The families of both young people were extremely close, and in trying to make sense of this tragedy, the victim's family reached out to the young man's family in order to share consolation and support. His family, however, would have none of it, convinced as they were of where responsibility for these crimes lay. The friend who told me this story was horrified at the degree to which the perpetrator's family held the young woman responsible for their son's crimes: "It's her fault; she treated him badly—the only thing he did wrong was love her too much and there's nothing wrong with love!" These kinds of confused sentiments are, unfortunately, common. Many continue to believe that dating and domestic violence are created by the victims of these crimes.

Domestic and dating violence are never a result of "loving too much." The highest levels of empathic concern, mutual respect, allowance of differences, and gentleness—perhaps above all else—characterize love. Those who confuse love with abuse profoundly distort the meaning of love into something synonymous with domination or control. Abuse is as far away from love as one can get.

Chapter Seven addresses the perplexing question of where to turn for assistance when those who are charged with helping only add, too frequently, to the problem. It provides a sobering look at the work of some of the most prominent authorities in the field of psychotherapy.

✦ ✧ ✦ **ACTION STEPS** ✦ ✧ ✦

FOR THE ACTION STEPS THAT FOLLOW, REFER TO THE LIST AT THE BEGINNING OF THIS CHAPTER TITLED "ABUSES OF POWER WITHIN INTIMATE RELATIONSHIPS" OR APPENDIX A: POWER AND CONTROL WHEEL.

✦ ✧ ✦ **ACTION STEPS** ✦ ✧ ✦
MEN

1. For each abuse of power listed (and appearing on the wheel) describe actions at the most benign or starting point of the continuum within that category. Male privilege, for example, often includes consistently second-guessing the decisions that women make instead of trusting their competence. Isolation often begins with a man expecting the woman he's dating to always spend her free time with him rather than in an activity she enjoys alone or with her friends. Emotional abuse often begins with "jokes" about a woman's appearance, profession, or friends.

2. If you are married, partnered, or in a dating relationship, con-sider whether your significant other would describe any of your behaviors as falling into the categories listed. If so, commit to doing what is necessary to start behaving in a *con-sistently* safe and respectful manner: schedule a consultation with a counselor trained in dealing with abusive relationships.

3. Watch for indications of abuse in the interactions you see between men and women and in the descriptions men share of their time spent with women.

4. When you observe abuse or hear a male family member, friend, or coworker describe interacting with a woman (or man) in a manner that seems abusive, tell him so and ask that he treat that person with greater respect. (Do not challenge another man in this way unless you see or hear him describe his own behavior. If you learn of his actions from his partner or a third party and then confront him, this likely will increase his abusiveness toward his partner.)

5. Pay attention to how it feels when you challenge another man in this fashion (and how it feels when you recognize abuse but decide to remain silent).

✦ ✧ ✦   **ACTION STEPS**   ✦ ✧ ✦

WOMEN

1. If you are married, partnered, or in a dating relationship, evaluate your relationship using the abuses of power listed (and appearing on the wheel). If you are single, evaluate previous relationships.

2. List any examples of your partner's patterns of behavior (and/or your own) that fall into each category of abuse.

3. If you currently find yourself on the receiving end of abuse within your relationship and it would not be safe to confront your partner, the National Domestic Violence Hotline, 800-799-7233, can direct you to the best local source of help. If you find yourself within an abusive relationship but do not feel physically endangered, seek assistance from a counseling professional trained in the dynamics of abuse. If there are no patterns of abuse within your relationship, congratulate yourself and your partner for the mutual respect that you show one another. If you are not currently involved in an intimate relationship, make a commitment to refer to the list of abuses of power (or power and control wheel) in order to keep safety and mutual respect the centerpieces of your next dating relationship.

✦ ✧ ✦ **ACTION STEPS** ✦ ✧ ✦
COUPLES

1. Referring to the list of abuses of power (or the power and control wheel), describe the decisions you each make daily that prevent abuse from occurring. Examples follow.

   ✧ A man decides to pay attention to which groceries are needed and the kids' activities schedules so that he doesn't fall into presuming that his wife will always take care of those matters. These decisions demonstrate love and respect for his wife instead of male privilege.

   ✧ Having witnessed threats, intimidation, and violent behavior by his grandfather toward his grandmother, one man decided early on that he would only touch the women he dated and the woman he married in ways that show caring, affection, and love.

✧ A woman remembers that her mother was required to ask her father before spending money on anything other than groceries. Refusing to be economically controlled by another person, this woman keeps her own savings and checking accounts apart from the joint account she and her husband keep for household expenses. She spends from her individually-held accounts according to her heart's desire.

2. Help each other identify decisions that they may be taking for granted:

✧ "You're a large man and you always decide to approach me and the children in a way that conveys openness and caring, never intimidation."

✧ "Like lots of guys, I'm not so clear at expressing how I'm feeling sometimes but you always give me a few minutes to get my thoughts and words together instead of putting me down."

✧ "If we disagree about how to manage something with one of the kids, you make a point of having that conversation privately instead of bringing them into the middle of it."

✧ "You always see sex as something for both of us. You never whine or pout if I'm exhausted and you're raring to go. You respect the way I'm feeling."

3. Thank each other for consistently treating each other with respect in a world that teaches otherwise.

7

Beware Therapists and Other "Helpers"

✦ ✧ ✦

Like everyone else in our society, mental health professionals, physicians, nurses, attorneys, police officers, judges, teachers, college professors, researchers, religious leaders, community leaders, and lawmakers grow up and live their daily lives within a social system that is saturated by beliefs, expectations, and guidelines for behavior that affirm mainstream cultural values, including the traditional male code. Consequently, helping professionals usually reinforce these values and expectations, whether unwittingly or purposely, in their work with families and individuals. It is vital that you keep this in mind when seeking assistance for relationship problems. Typically, professional helpers do one or more of the following:

✦ Treat behavior that is consistent with the male code as though it is normal, even "natural," and, therefore, not a problem despite the negative impact such behavior may be having upon others.

+ Expect women to assume more than half of the responsibility for making changes or accommodations necessary to sustain couple relationships.
+ Expect women to carry the bulk of responsibility for childcare, eldercare, and all other family and community related responsibilities.
+ Minimize the seriousness of abusive behavior committed by white men.
+ Expect female victims, rather than the male perpetrators of the violence committed against them, to take action to either make the violence stop or create safety in some other manner.
+ Minimize differences in a way that pretends everybody shares the beliefs, values, access to resources, and expectations generally associated with people who are white, heterosexual, male, without disabilities, and from middle- or upper-middle class backgrounds.

Therapists and other helping professionals reinforce these mainstream ideas and values to varying degrees. When a heterosexual couple seeks counseling, typically the woman takes the initiative, more ready to assume responsibility for change than the man. Many therapists go along with this, asking more of the woman and allowing the man to assume another role, less like a therapy client and more like a cheerleader or supporter for his partner. At the most extreme point on the continuum of collusion with male entitlement is the work of the psychiatrists and other mental health professionals who concocted Parent Alienation Syndrome (PAS). This new "diagnosis" is used to prevent battered women from protecting their children from exposure to their violent fathers. PAS asserts that children who resist parental visitation are not legitimately seeking protection from their fathers but instead have been "alienated" from their fathers by their mothers. PAS has been resoundingly discredited by ethical researchers and practitioners.

The message of this chapter: to never assume that the helping professional you decide to see recognizes the ways that power imbalances, male entitlement, and the traditional male code shape what goes on within couple and family relationships. Instead, assume that the therapist more than likely colludes with these patterns. Be ready to challenge them, and be ready to seek another therapist. This chapter provides examples of the work done by therapists who collude with male entitlement. It draws examples from my professional experience as well as from the writing of several of the most prominent authorities in the field of family therapy.

At a recent family therapy conference I attended, a presenter showed a videotaped therapy session in which a white middle-class man and woman, recently separated and trying to build a solid co-parenting relationship, were meeting with the presenter, a white female therapist. The woman, Stephanie, who was the primary custodial parent, voiced doubts about her parenting skills. She worried that her busy work schedule prevented her from giving enough time, love, and support to the couple's five-year old son, Peter. The little boy attended kindergarten, and by all accounts, was adjusting as well as could be expected to the recent changes in his family's structure.

The therapist listened carefully to Stephanie as she described her fears that the father's departure from the home made Peter feel insecure and fearful regarding the dependability of both parents. As the dialogue continued, it became evident to us conference participants that this mother, from everything we saw, was a thoughtful and loving parent. She put a great deal of time and emotional energy into being considerate, responsive, and thorough in addressing her son's needs.

The father, Joshua, who looked after his son for one night during the week and every other weekend, experienced no self-doubt regarding his parenting. Instead, he praised both himself and his former wife as exemplary parents, encouraging her to "give yourself a break and recognize what a great mother you are!"

The therapist had been presented with a wonderful opportunity to help both parents examine the gendered pattern they were enacting. The man, who indeed seemed a loving and involved parent, had no difficulty claiming kudos for his fathering. The woman, on the other hand, even though she put in far more parenting time and energy than did the man, found it impossible to rest assured that she was giving enough to their son. Instead of emphasizing this imbalanced pattern and helping both partners explore how it was likely the result of gender socialization, the therapist instead characterized the woman's uncertainty as pathological anxiety, hypothesizing the existence of a self-esteem problem.

Some conference attendees challenged the therapist's hypothesis, encouraging her to imagine the way gender socialization, as well as other social pressures connected to race and social class, was contributing to the differences between the experiences of this woman and man. One attendee asked, "Why are you so ready to pin a diagnosis on this woman? It seems to me that you let the man completely off the hook. I mean, he only sees his kid a fraction of the time that the mother does and yet he feels like he's father of the year. Didn't you wonder even a little about his lack of worry regarding the very real likelihood that his little boy was feeling abandoned by him? Did you wonder even a little if maybe the dad ought to be diagnosed with something—maybe narcissism or grandiosity or, at the very least, limited empathy?"

The therapist had difficulty responding to these challenges. Like too many other therapists, she had been indoctrinated into a willingness to accept gendered imbalances like the ones demonstrated by her client couple as normal. She seemed eager to identify individualized forms of pathology within women clients.

Let's look at examples from the published work of some prominent therapists. William O'Hanlon-Hudson and Patricia Hudson-O'Hanlon, in their 1995 book, *Love is a Verb: How to Stop Analyzing Your Relationship and Start Making it Great*, describe the following case. Patricia ("Pat") is the therapist.

> Dave and Laurie were at an impasse . . . Dave wanted Laurie to be more adventuresome sexually. To Dave, being "sexually adventuresome" meant having anal sex. Pat suggested they look at the category "more adventuresome about sex" and find what other actions they could agree upon. Laurie was modest . . . she decided she would be willing to be more adventuresome sexually by wearing a teddy, a garter belt, and hose. While this didn't completely meet Dave's desires, it gave him the message that she cared about his sexual desires and was willing to try some different behaviors to spice things up.

The solution that Pat gave to this couple falls right into line with Rules # 6 ("Be dominant!") and 7 ("Women are for sex!") of the traditional male code. The therapist accepts Dave's definition of the problem uncritically, affirming his dominance by not even exploring Laurie's definition. The therapist also presumes that the couple's sexual conflict can be addressed without considering other dimensions of the relationship that reveal power dynamics, such as how other conflicts have been negotiated, how joint decisions are made, whether or not each partner feels entirely safe to disagree with the other, how secure each partner is financially, and the extent to which each partner feels loved and listened to by the other. Instead of assessing these dimensions of the relationship, the solution proposes that Laurie move as far as she's willing toward giving Dave what he desires sexually.

Laurie's experience of Dave's push for more sexually adventuresome behavior remains unexamined. If Laurie were allowed to raise her definition of the problem and her experience of Dave's demands, she might have said something like, "Dave pushes me to participate in sexual behavior that I'm not comfortable with. He calls it 'adventuresome,' but I'm not aroused at all by the things he suggests, and it bothers me that this doesn't seem to register. Also, he doesn't seem much interested in learning more about what makes me feel good. The way he keeps pushing makes me feel like he's treating me like an object instead of his partner."

Imagine the circumstances reversed such that the problem this couple brings to Pat is Laurie's displeasure with Dave's reluctance to allow her to penetrate him anally using her favorite sex toy. Do you think Pat would be cajoling "modest" Dave toward getting a little more in line with Laurie's idea of being "sexually adventuresome?" I don't think so. It is doubtful that the therapist would consider encouraging Dave to accept Laurie's desires because most therapists, like most people in our society, affirm Rule #6 ("Be dominant!"), which assigns men a dominant role in partnerships. Therefore, many therapists would never expect a heterosexual man to consider accepting what most people consider a "submissive" sexual role. Indeed, because of the association between anal sex and gay sexuality, most therapists, in keeping with rule #8 ("Don't be gay!") would never consider supporting Laurie's request. Instead, they would likely consider Laurie's desire to have anal sex with Dave pathological and subject to pejorative examination.

To place this issue within an even broader and more unfortunate context, most therapists, like most everybody else in our society, expect women to compromise in all aspects of partnerships, even when the compromise is likely to make the woman feel uncomfortable.

In a second case described in *Love is a Verb*, the traditional male code once again receives unquestioning support:

> One couple Pat worked with discovered that they had completely different ideas about giving and receiving love. Jamal was very romantic and believed that love was demonstrated by things like surprise picnics and candlelit dinners. His wife, Denise, thought that Jamal could show her love by helping with the housework, arranging to have wallpaper hung in the family room, and cleaning his whiskers out of the bathroom sink after he shaved. Once they accepted that neither of them had *the correct* view of what love really is, each could begin to give love in a way that he or she recognized.

"Romantic" Jamal believed that love means surprise picnics and candlelit dinners. But what about Denise, whose vision of love included wistful dreams of her partner helping her with housework and home decorating, and, in addition to all that, also somehow managing to clean up the bathroom sink after using it? Before you go asking, "Could this woman's good possibly be any smaller?" try to imagine what might account for this disparity. Why might one partner reach for romance while the other would settle for a little help with the household chores and the willingness to clean up after oneself in the bathroom—a degree of responsibility-taking most of us would expect from anybody over the age of six?

It's likely that Jamal's and Denise's wildly divergent images of love speak volumes about the way power and privilege are organized and enacted within their marriage. A more responsible approach by the therapist would have included questioning this couple more deeply to find out why Jamal's visions of love center on his own pleasure and Denise's lean toward shared home responsibilities.

A woman friend of mine recently shared with me an exchange that occurred between her and her husband. She was about to turn thirty-five and her husband asked, "What would you like for your birthday?" My friend responded, "Truthfully, the best gift you could give me would be to remove your six coats from the living room chair like I've been asking you to do for the past month." She went on to say, "He just doesn't get it. I've been asking him forever to clean up after himself, if not for me then so at least he won't be setting such a bad example for the kids. He got pissed off about the way I answered his question about my birthday present, but I was telling the God's honest truth. It's really come to that! He's worn me down to the point where even just acting like a responsible housemate would be something special."

This situation may be very similar to what was going on between Jamal and Denise. How simple it would have been for Pat to ask questions that would reveal the power dynamics within this relationship. My first choice in this case would be, "Can you tell me how household chores are divided between the two of you and how this arrangement was arrived at?" In this and the previous example from her book, Pat, like many therapists, overlooks the power dynamics that have so much to do with the issues raised by her client couples. In doing so, she leaves male entitlement and male domination undisturbed and intact.

In John Gray's "Men are from Mars, Women are from Venus" book series, gender differences are strongly emphasized, but the power differences connected to gender, as well as those connected to differences of race, socioeconomic class, and sexual orientation, are obscured. The resulting framework emphasizes gender differences as naturally occurring phenomena with a neutral value. Gray encourages each gender to gain a better understanding of the other gender so there can be enhanced cross-gender relating. Focused squarely on communication and mutual understanding as the basis for successful partnerships, this approach leaves people like Denise in the above example without any validation or support regarding their need for gaining equal access to power and rights within their intimate relationships.

Michael Nichols, in *The Lost Art of Listening*, presents a perspective on relationships that also affirms traditional gender patterns. He offers the following as an example of a "successful" negotiation between a husband and wife:

> Wendy told Hank that she needed more help chauffeuring the kids to all their activities. He agreed. But Wendy went further and said, "I know you don't feel like it, otherwise you'd volunteer more often. When do you feel *least* like driving?" Hank really appreciated this consideration of his feelings. (Feeling like it's OK to say no made it a lot easier to say yes.) He said he didn't mind taking the kids places on weekends or early in the evening but he hated going out after nine on work nights. He also mentioned that it's a lot easier for him if he knows a day in advance that he has to drive them somewhere.

I find myself considering an array of questions, all of which go unattended by Nichols. Why is this negotiation organized so one-sidedly around Hank's desires? Isn't he also the parent of these children? If so, why is his parenting seemingly done on a "volunteer" basis? Why does he always have the option to decline, an option Wendy clearly does not have? Why is Wendy expected to know the kids' schedules and keep Hank informed "a day in advance?" Instead, why isn't Hank taking responsibility for knowing the kids' schedules as well as Wendy does? It seems that this couple, in accordance with Rule #1 ("Don't act like a girl!"), accepts that parenting and childcare fall under "women's work," and are therefore entirely Wendy's responsibility. The therapist appears to be in absolute agreement with this position, despite the obvious fact that the arrangement places Wendy in a grossly overly responsible position when compared to the children's other parent, Hank.

As the previous examples illustrate, even when therapists do acknowledge differences connected to gender, these differences remain acceptable and unquestioned as though they are a fact of nature, rather than socially-agreed-upon conventions that coincide with unequal access to power and privilege, and therefore beg to be dismantled.

When it comes to addressing abusive behavior, the field of psychotherapy has performed quite badly, more often than not colluding with offenders. Focusing almost exclusively on communication patterns, as they've generally been taught to do within their masters and doctoral psychology, social work, and counseling degree programs, many therapists practice while totally unprepared to deal responsibly with domestic and dating violence. They simply do not identify abuse as a significant issue, even when it is discussed openly or enacted right before their eyes during a consultation session. Instead, they either discount evidence of abuse as "not the real issue" or assume that the responsibility for abuse rests equally with both parties. In each of these cases, issues of unequal power, privilege, and entitlement go unexamined. The result generally causes people on the lesser end of the power scale to experience continued and often escalated suffering, while those who abuse their power are not held accountable or challenged to make changes—indeed, they often experience the therapy as an affirmation of their right to control their partner.

In the following example from his book, *The Lost Art of Listening*, family therapist Michael Nichols discards the importance of power differences between males and females even as he acknowledges the effectiveness of a man's hostile, intimidating behavior in controlling his wife's expression of her thoughts and feelings. In a bizarre sleight of hand, he seems to be suggesting that the most important thing to focus on when a man abuses his partner is not holding him accountable for his behavior that is causing pain to others, but rather encouraging him to explore his own history of painful feelings. Note the following case description.

> I soon found out why Sheila hesitated to protest. Once she said, "Don't you think you're being a little unfair?" and Lenny flew into a rage. He started shouting at her . . . it was awful . . . The same thing happened every time Sheila said anything critical to Lenny . . . Others might say '. . . Lenny's lashing out (is) typical of (his) gender. In fact these inferences are so general and judgmental as to constitute virtually meaningless clichés. For a more subtle appreciation of a person's overreactions we need to know their triggers . . . Lenny was filled with deep and ugly fears of worthlessness . . .

Consistent with Rule # 1 ("Don't act like a girl!"), which prioritizes males over females, Nichols prioritizes the pain Lenny feels inside over the pain he causes others. He also trivializes Lenny's abusiveness by calling it "overreaction." It might be an overreaction if Lenny "flew into a rage" one time during several years of marriage, showed remorse, and then transformed that remorse into a lived-out commitment to behave in a manner that thereafter caused Sheila to always feel safe and respected while in his company. But Nichols reports that this sort of thing happened "every time Sheila said anything critical to Lenny." Such being the case, it is fair and reasonable to label Lenny's pattern of "lashing out" a tactic of abuse.

Many leading therapists go even further than Nichols in their skewed attitude, analysis, and assignment of responsibility for behavior within couple interactions. These therapists directly blame victims for the assaults they suffer.

While supervising a case involving a husband who has frequently and severely beaten his wife, Jay Haley, one of the founders of the family therapy field, tells therapist and co-author David R. Grove:

> You described an incident that I bet is a metaphor for the history of their marriage. She leaves; 45 minutes later he leaves, and she's waiting for him. I bet they have a pattern where she leaves and then comes back. She leaves and yet tempts him. That is part of the violence.

Another example of this kind of understanding on the part of therapists, from Harville Hendrix's self-help book, *Keeping the Love You Find: A Guide for Singles*, follows:

> In many abusive families, there appears to be a victim and a tormentor . . . the man who beats his wife and then children, while she cowers in the corner and silently comforts her children when it is over. It seems easy to fix the blame in these situations, but this is dangerously misguided. It takes two to create this warped ballet. What is rarely acknowledged is that the battered wife knows only one way—the way she learned from her own mother—to get attention, and that is to provoke her distant, silent husband with relentless, though perhaps subtle, criticism, complaints, and rejection— until he explodes.

Instead of acknowledging and countering the entrapment created by abusive men who employ coercive tactics, this approach collaborates with batterers. The result is that battered women become re-assaulted within the very process that is supposed to help them gain safety.

While no further examples are probably needed to drive the point home, these last few bear inclusion because they shed light on the degree to which some white male heterosexual therapists, paying homage to Rules #1 ("Don't act like a girl!") and #8 ("Don't be gay!") of the male code, feel entitled to belittle women (as well as gay men).

Michael Nichols gives his attitude away in the following excerpt, which was meant, I imagine, to introduce humor into his discussion.

> When I complain to my friends about my wife nagging me to take out the garbage, it's just because my wife doesn't understand why I don't always feel like doing it. Besides, if I tried to discuss this directly with her, we might get into tedious and unnecessary issues, like fairness and inequality and so on.

Similarly, Frank Pittman, in *Man Enough: Fathers, Sons and the Search for Masculinity*, repeatedly employs sarcastic humor to embellish his points, and his statements frequently denigrate women as well as people who are gay, lesbian, bisexual, or transgender.

> Most women realize their femininity is an act they go into to control men without scaring them . . . Men who escape women, or seduce them, or silence them, or even beat and murder them are doing so not because they sadistically enjoy beating a woman—a feminist

stereotype of men's motives—but because they feel weak, burdened with a sense of imperfect masculinity.

Another way men have protected themselves from the power of women is to keep them too busy to stir up much trouble.

> The least a guy can do to pay back a gal who has down-pedaled her own career and tended to him and their kids, while letting him have all the fun of devoting himself to the selfish pleasures of work, is to make sure she gets to blow the money. If he can make her feel it is her money as much as his, she'll feel more nearly equal and will probably take better care of the money and better care of him.

Pittman describes a conversation he was part of while working out at the gym:

> One man said, "I've know homosexuals who were big and strong and could beat your ass." The other boys agreed that only heterosexuals could be real men, but they weren't too sure, and then they were sorry that such an unpleasant topic had been brought up.

This sort of joking from heterosexual white men who are among the most visible and widely-published family therapists speaks volumes about the largely destructive sensibilities still dominating the field.

Too many therapists, both male and female, continue to offer assistance for difficulties within couple relationships in ways that affirm power imbalances between the genders, male entitlement, and the rules of the male code. Similarly, too many therapists disregard differences connected to race, disability status, and sexual orientation, applying a one-size-fits-all approach to helping their clients. As the examples discussed earlier in this chapter illustrate, both of these unfortunate realities result in therapy that often does nothing to identify and challenge the power imbalances at the foundation of couples' problems. Instead, what happens is that one or both partners (usually the woman in a heterosexual couple) are encouraged to accept a label denoting mental illness, followed by "treatment" directed toward alleviating their symptoms. In addition, when couple difficulties have escalated to the level of abuse, therapists often behave in a manner that makes the problems worse, not better, increasing the threat of danger for domestic violence survivors.

OTHER PROFESSIONALS

Therapists are not the only helpers whose assistance often increases rather than mitigates the difficulties that couples and families experience. Family members, friends, community leaders, teachers, and health care providers too often fall into this category as well.

I once treated a white couple, John and Barbara, both of English-American background, who came to see me because of difficulty managing the behavior of their ten-year-old son, Fred. Fred bullied his six-year-old brother, Kevin, but behaved toward his three-year-old sister, Jennifer. John, a large and muscular man, stood six-foot-three and well over 200 pounds. Barbara was tiny, probably no taller than five feet.

Ten-year-old Fred not only acted domineering toward his brother, but also toward his mother, increasingly testing the limits she set for him by saying things like, "I don't have to listen to you because you're a girl." This behavior was peculiar to Fred, as Kevin and Jennifer minded both parents exceptionally well. Fred never disrespected his father.

As with all couples, my assessment included individual meetings with Barbara and John to look at the manner in which dimensions of power and control were organized within their relationship. This proved to be a substantially egalitarian relationship where both partners negotiated differences in a loving, respectful, and fair manner.

I provided coaching on effective parenting, including firm and consistent assignment of reasonable consequences and recognition for positive behaviors—simple, straightforward pointers for parents who seemed, on the whole, to be managing their reasonably well-behaved brood quite well. Barbara and John gratefully applied these suggestions and shortly thereafter reported that Fred was doing much better and treating all family members, including his mother and Kevin, with due respect.

At the point where it seemed to me that the family would soon be ending therapy, Barbara requested an additional individual session. While we had looked into her family of origin briefly during previous discussions, she now invited me into a more in-depth exploration of her family's history. "We've been real successful at helping Fred get more into line in terms of recognizing my authority, but I've still got so much fear about him—and I think I've figured out what it's all about," she began. "I think I'm so worried about him because he's the oldest son in our family and my brother, the oldest and only son in my family—you know, the family I grew up in— well, there was just a lot to worry about there." Barbara went on to tell me that her brother, who is three years older than his next oldest sister and five years older than Barbara, had sexually abused each of his three younger sisters over the course of many years.

To make a long and ugly story somewhat shorter and more focused, I went on to learn, through additional meetings with Barbara, along with her sisters, brother, parents, and in-laws, that her brother's sexually predatory behavior had come at various times to the attention of numerous people, none of whom had worked to hold him accountable in any significant way. These people included his parents, who barely even feigned surprise at the family meeting at which the three sisters each read a letter to their brother describing the impact of his offenses upon their lives and the lives of their children and partners. At this meeting, the offender's father revealed that his son had been "caught by his soccer coach when he was fourteen groping an eight-year-old girl." When I asked what the father and coach had done about it, he responded, "I just told him to stop it." He went on to explain, "When it comes right down to it, a stiff penis has no conscience." Perhaps this was his updated version of "Boys will be boys"?

I was surprised to learn that the offender, Mark, was "in counseling" with a Christian minister. Mark, to his credit, had informed the minister about abusing his sisters, and wanted to make amends for the pain he had created. The minister, who met with him weekly, advised a combination of prayer and weekly counseling discussions, but made no effort to direct Mark toward any reparative work with his sisters. Furthermore, and more ominously, the minister had not, during more than two years of counseling, explored any further the history and current status of Mark's predation. Mark was at that time the father of twin two-year-old baby girls. I assisted the minister and Mark in proactively making contact with the state offices that need to be informed of such matters, as I would need to do myself if they did not agree to follow through. Further evaluation revealed no indication of Mark assaulting his children or other children.

Now let's get back to Barbara, John, and their kids. Disclosing the secret in her family helped Barbara and her sisters make a demand for reparations, starting with Mark paying for their therapy. Barbara and John felt the grief and exhaustion that would predictably follow such an ordeal, but Barbara's vague fears about Fred went away. Now she had the desire to use her family of origin's history in a positive manner.

She and John decided to let all the kids know about Uncle Mark's abuse of his sisters. Together, they told this story to their kids using age-appropriate language and terms fitting their level of understanding. They used the story to highlight everybody's right to respectful touching and the need for each child to know their resources for support if anybody, including family members, ever touches them in a way that is not respectful, as well as their responsibility to touch others only in ways that are wanted and respectful. "Whenever you touch another person, that touch should make them feel cared for, not hurt," John explained to his children.

The previous example illustrates the ways that family, community members, and even professional helpers too frequently dismiss the significance of abusive behavior committed by males. In a complementary fashion, the world often conspires to deny females the support and assistance that would help them establish safety and justice for themselves and their children.

The story of a dear friend of mine provides many examples. Cyndie is a thirty-five-year old mother of four sons who has dark red hair and a mischievous Irish smile. Her favorite expressions are, "Hey, I ain't messin' around," and, "Work with me, people," both delivered with mock exasperation. She has a knack for loudly finishing my sentences with some off-color slam that's close to what I might have been thinking but a lot more fun.

Cyndie survived a decade of domestic violence and now collaborates with me on delivering domestic violence training at locations across the United States. Within these training sessions, she bares some of her most painful truths, sharing her personal story of survival in the face of being routinely beaten and tortured during ten years of marriage. Using statistics and research, she contextualizes her life experiences within the larger story of the international oppression of women. And she never backs away from a question.

"Yes, I had three children with him," Cyndie answers the disbelieving young male questioner. Fixing her eyes unapologetically on his, she adds, "During slave times black women raised families and some mothers even gave birth during the Holocaust. Women even manage to bear and raise kids after they've suffered genital mutilation. Can you imagine the danger I faced if I suggested he wear a condom? If I bought birth control pills—not that we had the money to buy both food and birth control pills— but if I bought birth control pills he probably would have killed me for 'being a slut.' He already screamed at me that I was a slut most of the times he beat the shit out of me! I tried to carry on as best I knew how during my period of captivity and this meant having and taking the best care possible of my kids." Invariably, at the end of her presentations, Cyndie is approached by one or more women whom she has inspired to move toward safety.

Before she was directed to the employee assistance program at her workplace, where she met a therapist named Terry who helped her get connected to resources that were ultimately effective in supporting her escape from her abusive marriage, Cyndie had lots of experience with helpers who were not at all helpful. She agreed to marry the man who became her husband, a man who had already been abusing her physically and emotionally for years, after becoming pregnant with his child. Her father believed marriage was the "right thing to do" despite his knowledge of the abuse she was suffering. Cyndie talks about how her father's notion of marriage as the "right thing to do" was actually more driven by an attempt to protect his reputation than by what he thought would keep her safe. She excuses him for this, however, commenting on his ignorance of the options and services that might have been more helpful.

When Cyndie's husband brutally raped her, she was strongly advised by hospital staff and police officers to reconsider filing charges, as the process of trying to prove rape would be an ordeal and was unlikely to yield a conviction. This event compounded her feelings of hopelessness and despair.

None of Cyndie's family members or friends knew of the existence of battered women's services, and this was during the late 1980s and early 1990s in a major metropolitan area where these services surely existed. Instead, those closest to her advised her to leave him, sometimes questioning her sanity for "putting up with him." None of them knew to inquire about the threats he had made about killing her younger siblings and parents if she tried to leave.

During three pregnancies and deliveries, never once was she questioned by her obstetrician regarding the safety of her marital home. Finally, when Cyndie visited a psychotherapist, the woman seemed emotionally overwhelmed by the stories Cyndie shared and at an absolute loss regarding how she might gain safety. Cyndie stopped seeing her after two visits because she didn't want to depress this "professional" any further.

Cyndie's stories are typical of what women who've experienced abusive relationships describe. Stories about religious leaders of all faiths are particularly plentiful, it seems. One woman recently described scheduling a private meeting with her imam to seek his help toward getting her husband to stop beating her. The imam chastised her for not adequately fulfilling her wifely duties in the areas of house-cleaning and laundry, predicting that things would get better as she became more proficient in these areas. Another woman reported reaching out to a deacon at her church in a desperate gambit for support. The next evening this deacon, accompanied by four of his peers, arrived at her home to have a discussion with her and her husband about the responsibilities of marriage. Predictably, after the deacons' departure the woman's husband beat her severely.

I do not mean to suggest that no valid help is available. Rather, I encourage you to evaluate any helping professional who is new to you. Trust your judgment. Ask any questions that will help you clarify uncertainties, and do not hesitate to get second opinions. Also, do not hesitate to end your relationship with a helping professional who does not treat you in a way that consistently feels respectful and fair. It is important to recognize that therapists are not immune to the bias present within the world, and to act accordingly for your own protection.

What are some of the markers that indicate fairness and respect? How can we work toward forging relationships that consistently embody these qualities? The following chapter offers suggestions.

✦ ✧ ✦ **ACTION STEPS** ✦ ✧ ✦
MEN

1. Identify a male helping professional whom you respect. He can be a healthcare provider, therapist, teacher, personal trainer, financial consultant, religious leader, politician, legal professional, work foreman/supervisor or other type of professional.

2. Write at least one example that describes a time you saw him interact with a man, woman, or child in a way that challenged the patriarchal male code. Make sure to describe the benefits that his actions created for those involved, and how things would have worked out differently if he had taken action that supported the patriarchal male code instead.

3. Discuss what you've written with at least one other man. If you feel comfortable doing so, bring your example to the attention of the man whom it's about—and thank him.

✦ ✧ ✦ **ACTION STEPS** ✦ ✧ ✦
WOMEN

1. Write an example from your own experience, or from the experience of a female friend or family member, that describes a time when a professional helper caused harm by supporting the patriarchal male code.

2. Describe what the person on the receiving end of this professional's actions might have done in order to protect herself, or might do if the situation reoccurred.

3. Make a commitment to respond in a self-protective manner should such a situation ever happen to you in the future.

4. Talk about your commitment with at least one close friend.

✦ ✧ ✦ **ACTION STEPS** ✦ ✧ ✦
COUPLES

1. Agree to watch for the kinds of disrespectful behavior described in this chapter when the two of you interact with healthcare and childcare providers, educators, salespeople, religious leaders, counselors of all types, and other helping professionals.

2. Commit to supporting each other in requiring fair and respectful treatment for both partners from such professionals, and follow through on this commitment.

8

Transforming the Male Code

✦ ✧ ✦

What do we men need to do in order to let go of the power of domination and embrace the power of love instead? As is often the case, the search for the solution begins with understanding the problem itself, the traditional male code. Based upon power as domination, this unofficial manual for men, this code, encourages us to behave in ways that grant us entitlement and power over others at the cost of countless lost opportunities for love. For us to build partnerships that demonstrate the power of love instead of the power of domination, the code needs a serious overhaul. More specifically, the restrictions that constitute the male code need to be transformed into affirmations. This chapter presents those affirmations.

The eight affirmations for men listed below are based primarily upon the work I've done with family therapy colleagues Roberto Font and Rhea Almeida. Consider the affirmations as an antidote to the eight traditional rules introduced in Chapter Three. Actually, this code of affirmations is not just for men. It is useful for people of all genders who strive to create relationships based upon love, equality, and justice.

Each rule of the male code listed in Chapter Three ends with an exclamation point because in our hearts and minds we hear them as orders, demands, and admonishments. There is a negative tone to their energy. They dominate us as they exhort us to dominate the world. Unlike the rules of the male code, the affirmations below are punctuated by periods. The energy within these statements feels calm and grounded. It doesn't come from demands or domination. Instead, the energy here comes from love. Consider these rules invitations toward deeper and more meaningful connections with yourself and others.

AFFIRMATIONS FOR MEN

AFFIRMATION 1: *People of all genders are equally valuable.*

AFFIRMATION 2: *The language of feelings is essential.*

AFFIRMATION 3: *My life is more important than my work.*

AFFIRMATION 4: *Asking for help is a good thing.*

AFFIRMATION 5: *I approach problems with openness and flexibility.*

AFFIRMATION 6: *Collaboration works better than domination.*

AFFIRMATION 7: *We are all human beings, not objects.*

AFFIRMATION 8: *I have the courage to fight against bias.*

A final word before moving forward: the ideas in this chapter may appear to be nothing more than common sense, and in fact I believe that in most cases that's exactly what they ought to be. The problem is not so much in the knowing but in the doing, however. As Monica McGoldrick, one of my family therapy mentors, once remarked, "There are some things about relationships that are hard to figure out, but most of the time it's not that way. Most often, what needs to be done to make things better is pretty straightforward and obvious. The hard stuff is actually doing it."

This chapter lays out some of those fairly obvious things that can be done differently to make relationships better. Meet the challenge and do them!

AFFIRMATION

1

People of all genders are equally valuable.

Two of my son's Little League coaches, both of whom are white, heterosexual men living middle- or upper-middle-class lives, exemplify this affirmation. Dave and John manage Erik and his seven- and eight-year-old "Yankees" teammates, two of whom are girls, with a skillful mixture of encouragement, limit-setting, and teaching acumen, all delivered with unfailing good humor.

Dave responded quickly at practice one evening when it came to the inevitable "You throw like a girl!" epithet hurled by a boy named Sebastian, perhaps the team's most consistently surly member. Sebastian had directed it at Charlie, who had blown a play at first base by throwing the ball three feet higher than Sebastian's outstretched glove.

Dave shouted to Sebastian, "Have you ever seen the girls' baseball team play, Sebastian? You'd be doing real well if you could throw as well as most of the girls on that team!"

Later, when they finished practicing, John said to the team, "Kids, it's important to be respectful to everybody on the team— and to be a good sport when it comes to other teams also. If somebody on our team makes an error, you can say something like 'nice try' to give them some encouragement. It's never okay to put anybody down. Also, keep in mind that we have boys and girls on this team, and people from all different kinds of background also. What do I mean by that?"

Becky answered, "Well, like my parents came from West Virginia and Dinesh's came from Pakistan?"

"That's exactly what I mean!" said John, smiling broadly at Becky. "So we all are different in some ways and that means we bring all kinds of great strengths to the team. That's what makes a team, people putting their different strengths together. The fact that we have both boys and girls on our team—and also kids from lots of different backgrounds—makes us a really strong team." With that said, he gave the kids a few more words of encouragement before they left for home with their parents.

In our everyday lives, valuing both femininity and masculinity means that men challenge themselves to embrace qualities and activities they've been taught to consider feminine and therefore off-limits. Dancing, cooking, reading and writing poetry, and creating and appreciating all forms of art fall into this category. Activities that men have generally avoided also include caregiving occupations like nursing, teaching, and childcare work. It's no coincidence that these women-identified occupations have been chronically undervalued and underpaid in our society, despite the level of skill they require and their vital importance to all families and communities.

Valuing women and girls requires us to engage in an even more continuous and significant challenge—to monitor the ways that we interact differently with women and girls than we do with other males. Do we listen more carefully to males than we do to females? Interrupt males less frequently? Value the ideas and contributions of males more highly? Solicit the advice and input of our male coworkers more readily? Your immediate response may be, "Of course not!" But watch yourself carefully for a few days from a brutally honest perspective, and you may well be surprised and disturbed by what you see.

One of the best strategies for making this affirmation a lived reality is getting together regularly with a group of men who are working toward the same goal. As has been mentioned a number of times previously, we men tend to listen most attentively to one another. We can use this fact to help us work toward change. I'll discuss this more within Chapter Nine.

AFFIRMATION 2

The Language Of Feelings Is Essential.

Most of us men are great at putting some of our emotions into words. We are well prepared (in some cases overly prepared) to tell you when we feel uncomfortable, annoyed, frustrated, irritated, angry, aggravated, mad, ticked off, teed off, pissed off, fuming, furious, outraged, and enraged. But just ask how we feel about the beautiful sunset unfolding on the horizon, and many of us will be hard pressed to pull two words together.

Each of us, people of all genders, relies upon our most familiar tools to manage our lives. You've probably heard the old adage that if all you have is a hammer, everything looks like a nail? Well, the same applies to the words we use to capture our emotions. Words are the only tools we have to make sense of how we're responding emotionally to everything that happens in our lives, from our current mood to the current state of our body's functioning to relationships with everybody with whom we come into contact to our relationship with the larger world around us. So if the emotional descriptors we men have been taught to be most comfortable with fall roughly into two main categories—those related to anger and those related to the benign, neutral emotional state we allow to capture most everything else—we're likely to decide that the emotion of the moment falls into one of these two possible categories. This is a simplification, of course, but the point is an important one. Predictably, the emotional restrictiveness that many men embrace as they identify with the traditional code sets them up for disconnection, misunderstanding, and lost opportunities within a multitude of relationships.

The challenge, therefore, dares one to become familiar with the entire range of emotional descriptors—to get a more complete set of tools, if you will. Expanding beyond the word anger, and "Everything is okay, I guess," one enters a world of words for an infinite palette of emotions, including all the subtle nuances of feelings like exuberance, joy, love, wonder, awe, fear, sadness, worry, remorse, disappointment, belonging, comfort, closeness, distance, and loneliness.

Why is skill at using "feeling words" so important? Because the words that identify feelings communicate the fabric of human understanding, empathy, and connection. The more clarity with which we describe our experiences, the more clarity with which we can make decisions about what is best for us to do within our relationships, and our world.

Let me give you an example. When my son, Erik, was six years old, we lived next door to a Southeast-Asian-American family, the parents having immigrated to the United States from India eight years earlier. Michael, the youngest child in the family, was Erik's buddy. One Saturday morning after Erik had visited with Michael, he came home looking a little downcast. I asked him to tell me what was going on.

"I don't know," he said, "but Michael's grandparents are there and almost everybody is speaking a different language than English."

I asked Erik how he felt about that.

"It makes me feel like I'm not welcome," he said.

Erik and I talked about the fact that Michael's grandparents had spent most of their lives in India and were more comfortable speaking Hindi than English, particularly inside their homes. I asked him what he thought it was like for them to live in their country, India, and yet be expected to speak English in many public places. He said that he didn't think that would feel very nice and that it would be important for them to be able to speak Hindi whenever possible. I asked him if there were any other things that went on in Michael's home that made him feel unwelcome.

His response was, "No, Michael and his family are really nice, his grandfather was even trying to teach me some of their words!"

I told him that I thought it would be a special gift for him to learn some Hindi words from Michael's grandfather, and that such an offer would make me feel very special, if I were him.

Erik was quiet for a few moments while he fiddled with his shoelaces. Finally he said, "You know, I don't think I felt so much unwelcome as kind of dumb, and I didn't like feeling dumb." He continued. "They all knew how to talk in that language and I didn't, so I felt like there was something not so good about me. Now I see that they were actually trying to make me feel welcome by teaching me some words . . . and that it's okay to not know how to speak their language because I grew up here and in our family we speak English." We talked a little bit more. Finally, he said, "Now I feel better, like I'm okay and it's really nice of them to try to teach me their words . . . they must really like me!" The next afternoon he eagerly shared the words with me that he had learned from Michael's grandfather earlier that day.

Erik has an unusually well-developed vocabulary (if I do say so myself!), and he's extraordinarily skilled at using feeling words. Consequently, he pinpointed his initial feeling as "unwelcome," and then, through exploratory discussion, redefined his feeling with even greater specificity into "kind of dumb." That description really fit for him. Once he identified the feeling precisely, he immediately began to check it out within the context of his relationships in the world. He knew immediately, for example, that it was unreasonable to expect that he would be able to speak Hindi, as he had always lived in the United States. Also, Erik quickly realized that Michael and his family were not trying to teach him "their words" because they were taking pity on this poor stupid child, but rather because this was a way to include him, to welcome him into their family's conversation.

Imagine if Erik's most familiar feeling words outside the "everything's okay, I guess" category had been in the realm of anger, as is so common with boys and men. He would have come home looking sullen. Upon inquiry, he probably would have said something like, "They made me angry" or, "I felt uncomfortable." It would have been impossible for him to have moved from there to a more complete understanding of what had happened without the availability of all the feeling words he had tried out: "unwelcome," "dumb," "not so good about himself"; and, as he thought it through more completely: "better," "okay about himself," and "liked."

These words helped Erik make better sense of what was going on in his relationship with Michael and Michael's family. More importantly, the words that lie outside the anger category helped him negotiate from a place where he felt disconnected from Michael's family to a place where he felt strongly connected to them.

Such is the case with all relationships. Familiarity with the whole palette of feeling words provides the vehicle for understanding one's relationship to self and others. For those who are uncomfortable or unfamiliar with the language of emotions, the key to growth is paying attention to one's feelings and trying out words. Ask yourself questions like, "Is that the best way to describe how I'm feeling or can I get even more specific?" and, "What other feelings do I have about this? (Usually there are a whole range of feelings arising from a single experience or event)." If you have difficulty moving beyond words related to anger or vague unspecified discomfort (sometimes described as anxiety), dig deeper. Often fear, disappointment, and feelings of vulnerability, confusion, and sadness underlie anger. Looking into these feelings can help you get to a place that feels more constructively connected to others. Finally, talking with people whom you trust and respect about how you feel and how they might feel in similar circumstances also helps in finding the appropriate words.

AFFIRMATION 3

My Life Is More Important Than My Work.

Heterosexual men who adhere to the traditional male code believe that the development and maintenance of personal relationships and non-work activities should be delegated to their girlfriend, wife, sister, mother, or some other female. This world view gives men responsibility for all things related to paid employment; and for everything else, their responsibility is limited mainly to deciding whether or not to show up. A dynamic is established whereby the unique and fleeting frustrations and joys of child-rearing, shared family times, and adventures with friends are subordinated to paid employment and, as a result, profoundly devalued. We have arrived at a culture, supported by the traditional male code, in which our work has taken absolute precedence over those aspects of our lives through which we might experience our full humanity: connections to the ones we hold most dear, the world of nature, and our spirituality.

Affirmation #3 challenges men to resist the unrelenting messages that encourage us to devote our lives primarily to working for money. Its message encourages us to build satisfying connections with other people, while keeping ourselves economically secure. I'm not suggesting that work is unimportant; instead, I'm advocating that the relative importance of work be re-evaluated so that it can be seen from a more balanced perspective. This requires a fundamental paradigm shift within which work becomes less a defining measure of ourselves and, instead, a means to the end of experiencing a full life.

This requires us to try out what may be new practices and skills: family event and vacation planning; the nurturing of friendships; and, for parents, juggling an endless stream of competing scheduling priorities such as soccer games, dentist appointments, school plays, business meetings, community development sessions, etc. Also within this mix may be the challenge of working toward and maintaining adult-to-adult intimacy with one special person—the opportunity to devote attention to the needs, wants, and desires of the one you hold most dear.

I have a friend and colleague who told me a story about one of the ways he shows love to his wife. Marty is a forty-five-year-old Italian-American man who's been married to his wife, Maria, for eighteen years. The couple has three sons, aged five to fifteen. "I know that Maria loves more than anything else to be close to her family," said Marty, "and she's particularly close to her mother." He went on, "So what I do is every few weeks I tell her I'd love to bring her mother and sisters over to spend Sunday with us. I go get her mom in Brooklyn and her two sisters in Queens and bring them to our place. I cook a big Italian meal—everybody's Italian—and we all just spend time talking and being together. Maria's on the phone to her mother and sisters all the time during the week but I know how good it feels to her to have them come over."

"Wow," I said, "That's great! It also sounds like a lot of work."

"Yeah, it is. It takes a fair amount of preparation, you know—cleaning the place up, planning dinner, and shopping," said Marty, "And, while I love her family, it's not what I'd call first choice for my weekend, but it just makes her so happy! Besides, Maria always tells me after we're alone together how much she appreciates what I've given to her. Nothing's better than that!"

You might imagine that the importance of building a life outside the workplace ought to be self-evident, but for many men, this isn't so. There's an old saying about how you never hear of a man voicing deathbed regrets about not having spent enough time at his workplace. The lesson within this adage remains one of life's most important and, unfortunately, most poorly heeded ones.

AFFIRMATION 4

Asking For Help Is A Good Thing.

This affirmation counters the traditional male emphasis on self-reliance with recognition of the vital importance of learning to ask for and utilize assistance from others. It turns on its head the typical male belief that asking for help is a sign of weakness and affirms it as a strength instead. The idea is such common sense, yet so strongly proscribed by the old male code, that it's a particularly hard one for many of us to enact.

An increasing number of men rise to the challenge, however, and seek help readily. Forty-two-year-old Jan, married and the father of two sons, came to see me because he felt preoccupied with upset feelings toward his four siblings.

"They offered no help after Josh was born five years ago and now they're too busy to help with Mom," said Jan.

Josh, who now enjoyed great health, had been born two months premature and remained in the hospital for several weeks. With their lives stretched between home and the preemie ward, Jan and his wife, Helen, depended upon friends and neighbors to help care for their younger son, Jake. All three of Jan's brothers and his only sister lived nearby, but not one of them offered assistance. Now Jan's mother had been diagnosed with Alzheimer's disease and his siblings showed little interest in this development.

"I came to see you because I can feel myself pulling away from Helen and the kids. The news about my mom's condition has brought back all the hurt I felt when my brothers and sister deserted us after Josh was born. I don't know what to do with how I feel about my family, and I don't know how to approach them. It's eating me up inside."

Nobody had prompted Jan to see a therapist. He later informed me that he contacted me because "when I need a computer technician, I call tech support—this time I needed a family technician."

Jan remains the exception to the rule. Many men feel something is wrong in their intimate partnership. Some are unhappy about a repetitive pattern they can't seem to break out of (gambling, substance abuse, time spent on the internet, or unprotected sexual activity, for example). Some worry about a persistent physical symptom, yet do nothing about it. Only when the problem becomes unavoidably large do they seek assistance. We need and deserve to treat ourselves better than this. Self-reliance is an admirable attribute, but not when rigidly applied. It needs to be balanced by the wisdom of knowing when to ask for and accept help.

5
AFFIRMATION
I Approach Problems With Openness and Flexibility.

Julie is a thirty-seven-year-old Irish-American who works as a director of marketing within a large corporation. She's also the mother of four sons, aged fourteen months to fourteen years. Julie and her partner, Chuck, recently worked through a problem together in a way that was an important learning experience for

Chuck. He is a thirty-five-year-old Polish-American man who works as the manager of a large department store.

The story began as follows. Julie's twelve-year-old, Warren, and his other Little League team members, were getting ready for an end of season game when their coaches gathered them together. They told the kids to throw the game so that the team they were playing that evening would be able to make it into the statewide series. If her son's team won the game, their town would not be represented in the statewide series. If her son's team lost the game, their town would be represented by the opposing team.

Word of what the coaches did got back to Julie and Chuck later that evening. Julie and Chuck were both appalled, feeling that the coaches were modeling all the wrong things. Little League, they agreed, is supposed to teach values like fair play and sportsmanship.

Recalling the moment, Chuck said, "I was so furious! It took all I had to hold myself back from finding those two idiots and punching their lights out. I mean it, I felt like that was the way to handle it!" He went on to say, "Thank God Julie, who was just as angry as I was, had some better ideas. She said we should check in with some of the other parents, see if their kids were telling the same story, and then figure out together what to do about it."

As it turned out, a number of the other kids had brought the matter to the attention of their parents. Following Julie's lead, the group asked to speak with the coaches. Unfortunately, the coaches denied their actions. When Julie, Chuck, and the other parents approached the local Little League authorities, they got no satisfaction. Unwilling to be ignored, the group wrote letters to Little League's national offices and to area newspapers. They felt it was important to hold these coaches accountable—that not doing so would send the wrong message to their sons. The matter got a fair amount of media attention, including newspaper articles, Julie's appearance on a national television news program, and an interview with *People* magazine.

"Julie showed great organizing and leadership skills," beamed Chuck. "I was so proud of her." He paused thoughtfully and continued in a more solemn tone, "If I had followed my first impulse, which was really strong—in fact, even later when the coaches denied what they'd said I really had to talk myself out of belting both of them—if it were all up to me, I'm pretty sure I would have made a bad mistake. I mean, just think about it, if I punched those guys out, what good would that do? It would probably make me feel like the self-righteous good guy for about two seconds and then what? I would've been up on charges! What would that have taught Warren and the other kids?"

Unfortunately, Chuck's initial "let's solve the problem by beating the crap out of someone" approach is the one that traditional male socialization backs up. As with the other traditional rules, the one about men solving problems using aggression is evident everywhere within our society.

Recall the U.S. government's response to the 9/11 tragedy, for example. The government's stated goal was to bring to justice the terrorists who were behind these atrocities, along with their accomplices. Commentators reflecting on the aftermath point out that the government of Afghanistan repeatedly offered to extradite Osama Bin Laden and others for trial if the U.S. provided evidence, as would be the usual expectation in any such international judicial matter. The U.S. government ignored these offers and rushed into war against Afghanistan. To date there have been hundreds of thousands of civilians and thousands of U.S. soldiers killed in both Afghanistan and Iraq, yet the original objective of detaining Osama Bin Laden goes unmet.

A speaker at a recent conference about the effect of 9/11 on families mentioned her profound disappointment and great sadness at the government's response to the atrocities. "When it became so clear that individuals were willing to sacrifice their lives in order to inflict horrendous pain upon U.S. citizens, our government seemed to respond primarily with aggression. If only our leaders could have been more thoughtful. Indeed, if only they could have kept within their deliberations a spirit of humility and concern for all people."

Anger is a vitally important emotion. It lets us know that we have been wounded or wronged. Anger can energize us toward protecting our integrity and security. When anger is enacted as aggression, however, the results almost always lead to more hurt for all concerned. Affirmation #5 challenges us to recognize the full range of options that are available for approaching the problems that confront us in life. From there, the challenge is to choose the options that are most likely to provide safe and constructive resolutions for all concerned.

AFFIRMATION

6

Collaboration Works Better Than Domination.

Gary is a fifty-two-year-old married Hawaiian-American man who manages a team of seven training development staff at a large corporation. "I'm a veteran of the U.S. Navy and I'm a veteran of Corporate America," he told me during our recent conversation. "I became more than a little tired of the command and control attitude that runs the show in both places." I had contacted Gary in the process of developing a mentoring program for managers. He was identified by his area's senior executive as one of her very best people managers.

"So how is your leadership style different from that?" I asked.

"It's not rocket science," Gary said with a smile. "All you really have to do is listen to people, find out where their passions and interests are, and help them be aware of the big picture goals and objectives; then you work with them to create our department's goals and objectives. From there, I just try to help all of us contribute together effectively . . . It's kind of corny, but I look at myself as sort of a team choreographer instead of a task master. Believing in my team's competence and trying to help them get their work done by removing obstacles as best I can—that's what works! Most important of all, you never want to trample on your group members' initiative and competence by being overbearing and by micromanaging. That makes people feel devalued, demoralized, and uncertain about their strengths."

Gary's idea about being a team choreographer, instead of a task master, is relevant to many situations both within and beyond the workplace. He transforms "power over"—the power of domination—into "power with"—the kind of power that has nurturing and responsibility toward others at its core.

When the shared desires for collaboration and consensus-building, instead of domination, characterize the power dynamics within an intimate relationship, a number of patterns are evident:

+ Both partners consistently behave in ways that are non-threatening.
+ Each partner feels free to express themselves regardless of whether or not their thoughts and feelings are consistent with those of their partner.
+ Each person listens respectfully and non-judgmentally to what the other has to say.
+ There is mutual trust and support.
+ Each partner feels empowered to identify their own feelings, aspirations, and dreams, believing that differences and conflicts—and there are

bound to be many whenever two people feel free to express their individuality—will be negotiated thoughtfully and with equal consideration for both individuals.

+ Both members of the couple feel free to associate with friends and participate in activities of their choosing.
+ Honesty and accountability are shared expectations.
+ The partners keep each other informed of all matters relevant to the couple or family's welfare, including the details of asset ownership, debt, and other financial matters; employment status; and health status.
+ Both parties accept responsibility for their behavior, admit when they are wrong, and demonstrate the willingness to make reparations.
+ Joint responsibilities are shared equitably, including child and elder care, household maintenance, and the making of all decisions whose outcomes affect both parties.

In summary, affirmation #6 challenges us to replace individual power and control with collaboration and consensus—the power of love.

AFFIRMATION 7

We Are All Human Beings, Not Objects.

As mentioned in chapter two, pornography has long been the sexuality primer for most males in our society. With the advent of video game technology and the prevalence of violent imagery within this media, the pornography many young men experience today is more interactive and more violent in nature than ever before. This unfortunate state of affairs challenges us to recover an awareness that real human-to-human contact involves two living, breathing, thinking, and feeling people instead of one person and a virtual or glossy image having no human vulnerabilities and needs.

In addition to the ways in which boys and men are generally taught to devalue women and girls (underlying most men's tendency to dehumanize those with whom we interact sexually) is our society's degree of comfort with dehumanizing people in general. We live in a society where mainstream values promote the commoditization of everything, including people, as well as every aspect of their lives and experiences. By commoditization I mean turning people into things that can be bought, sold, disposed of, and, overall, treated as though they are objects.

I recently facilitated a "Change Management" workshop for a group of technology professionals whose area had suffered the loss of several coworkers through a "downsizing." The group struggled to make sense of the justification offered by their senior management for the reduction in force. Senior management had explained to them that by moving some of their group's work to India, the company would benefit because contracting for services in Southeast Asia was less expensive than using domestic employees. It had apparently seemed self-evident to the senior executive making this statement that "benefiting the company" was an inarguably noble objective. He had been caught off guard, though, when one of the workshop's participants had asked him to explain further.

This participant asked, "What do you mean by 'The company will benefit'? . . . All of us in this group ARE the company and the people you just let go ARE the company too, and I don't think even one of us sees the benefit in you taking away the jobs of our friends and coworkers. What's more, you're basically telling us that the rest of us are next, as soon as you can line up more contracted services in Asia to take over the work our remaining group members are doing." The executive had responded with a vague statement about how the company needed to focus on "shareholder value" and that "no further cuts were planned."

As we talked about this exchange, the group decided that they are considered by business leaders not as members of the company, i.e., people who take pride in their contributions to their shared accomplishments while also relying upon their wages to support families, but rather commodities, i.e., relatively expensive *things* currently necessary to ensure production. We went on to discuss how this mentality, while profoundly dehumanizing, is also entirely normal within our society.

Another example of our society's penchant for reducing people to objects occurred during a segment on CBS *Sixty Minutes* television news magazine in which TV journalist Lesley Stahl interviewed then-Secretary of State Madeleine Albright. During this interview, Sec. Albright indicated that the hundreds of thousands of children who had died in Iraq as a direct result of UN-imposed sanctions had been a reasonable price to pay for the supposed gains to United States security.

Living within a society that reduces people to things while also teaching boys that they are better than girls and that men's sexual partners should be approached as objects sets up major challenges for people of all genders. We must re-humanize our understanding of one another in sexually intimate relationships, as well as in all other kinds of relationships.

So what does it look like when one values the humanity of one's sexual partner? In very simple terms, it means we demonstrate that we recognize our partner as a human being. Empathy, mutual respect, kindness, communication, and generosity of spirit are some of the keys that make this happen. With these factors present, sexual intimacy becomes an experience within which sexual gratification happens, but one participant's gratification is not won at the other's expense, or as a result of domination. When both partners experience physical gratification delivered in an envelope of empathic connection, sexual expression becomes one of the means whereby they recognize and celebrate their shared humanity. As we'll discuss further within Chapter Nine, men have the opportunity to foster this rehumanizing of sexual relationships by being role models to one another and to boys in ways that support such a viewpoint.

AFFIRMATION

I Have The Courage To Fight Against Bias.

Traditional masculinity depends upon a collection of biases, most notably against women and gay men. Manliness, in other words, has been defined in opposition to femininity and gay sexual orientation. But it doesn't end there. Mainstream American culture stereotypes some racial and ethnic groups as "less manly" than others. And the implied question, "What kind of a man must he be if he can't make enough money to feed his family?" assaults men of lower socioeconomic groups.

Affirmation #8 challenges us to work toward dismantling all the biases that support hierarchies of domination. Doing so expands our definition of masculinity to include the valuing of people of all genders, sexual orientations, ethnicities, skin colors, disability statuses, and class backgrounds. The effort to dismantle the biases we've absorbed from the world, as the following story from my own experience illustrates, is much easier said than done, despite the fact that many of us may like to believe we are already there.

My partner, Tim, and I attended a holiday party in December, 2000, where we talked with Steve and Debbie, a middle-aged, professional white couple with whom we reconnect every year at this holiday event and whom we generally have no contact with otherwise. We were marveling at the ongoing electoral circus featuring George W. Bush and Al Gore.

Steve turned to me and said, "Well, you know I'm not homophobic and I hope you don't mind me asking, but what's the gay perspective on Bush's election?"

I paused for a moment while I puzzled over his statement. "Steve," I said cautiously, "what do you mean you're not homophobic? How could you not be homophobic? I mean, how could anybody who's grown up in this country not be even a little bit homophobic? I'm even homophobic and I'm gay." The gathering defensiveness in Steve's eyes seemed to melt into a look of slightly confused interest. I continued. "Yeah, sometimes I say to myself, 'whoa—you're sleeping with a man—what is THAT about?' And then I have a little talk with myself to challenge the self-hatred I've soaked up from the world. Saying you're not homophobic is like saying you're not racist or sexist. The way I see it, we all need to work at getting rid of those hateful things that we've taken into ourselves, but I won't deny for a minute that it's still a struggle."

After a pause in the conversation, Steve said, "I . . . I . . . I guess I'll have to give that some thought."

At the time, I had thought briefly about letting Steve know how unsettling it had felt when he asked me to speak for the "gay perspective," as though it would be reasonable to ask a gay, Latino, or female person to speak for their whole group, but I let him off the hook. At the next year's party though, I remembered to ask him for the heterosexual perspective on President Bush's first year in office.

Whereas traditional notions of masculinity assert that "real men" are not anything like women and gay men, and, further-more, that "real men" are financially successful, a transformed notion of masculinity may one day assert that "real men" embody the best qualities humanity has to offer. These include being emotionally present, connected, empathic, and expressive—pat-terns of behavior traditionally deemed feminine. Also included in this expanded definition of masculinity may be the idea that "real men" are loving, caring, understanding, and nurturing toward other men—patterns of behavior traditionally avoided by many men for fear others might perceive them as gay. Finally, and perhaps most importantly, we may one day arrive at a definition of masculinity that defines "real men" as those who courageously struggle to extend fairness, safety, and equal opportunity to everybody.

The affirmations in this chapter offer a vision for relationships in which the power of love replaces the power of domination. They belong to a time in the future, as we still have a long way to go. Getting there will require courage, creativity, persistence, and mutual support. Most important of all, it will require the par-ticipation of men. Because we men find ourselves at the center of the problem, we are uniquely positioned to work toward cre-ating solutions. Chapter Nine provides examples of how we can move this work forward.

✦ ✧ ✦ ACTION STEPS ✦ ✧ ✦

REFER TO THE AFFIRMATIONS BELOW FOR THE ACTION STEPS THAT FOLLOW.

AFFIRMATION 1: *People of all genders are equally valuable.*
AFFIRMATION 2: *The language of feelings is essential.*
AFFIRMATION 3: *My life is more important than my work.*
AFFIRMATION 4: *Asking for help is a good thing.*
AFFIRMATION 5: *I approach problems with openness and flexibility.*

AFFIRMATION 6: *Collaboration works better than domination.*
AFFIRMATION 7: *We are all human beings, not objects.*
AFFIRMATION 8: *I have the courage to fight against bias.*

✦ ✧ ✦ ACTION STEPS ✦ ✧ ✦
MEN

1. Copy the list of affirmations above and keep it with you for easy reference—in your wallet, car, or tacked near your desk or work station.

2. Consider the challenges posed by each affirmation. The following questions may help:

   ✧ Will living this affirmation make me stand out in a way that feels uncomfortable?
   ✧ Will my work supervisor disapprove?
   ✧ Will someone think I'm weak?
   ✧ Will anyone question my manhood?

   Strategize about how you'll muster the courage to meet these challenges.

3. Make a commitment to enact a number of the affirmations during the upcoming week. Identify specific actions that you'll take.

4. Take a few minutes every day to review actions you took during the last 24 hours that demonstrated one or more of the affirmations.

5. List the resulting benefits to others and/or yourself, and describe how these benefits add to the amount of love in your life.

✦ ◇ ✦ **ACTION STEPS** ✦ ◇ ✦
WOMEN

THE AFFIRMATIONS LISTED ABOVE ARE MORE OFTEN PRACTICED BY WOMEN THAN MEN—AND WOMEN OFTEN TAKE THEIR EMBRACE OF THESE AFFIRMATIONS FOR GRANTED. I ENCOURAGE YOU TO ACKNOWLEDGE, VALIDATE, AND CELEBRATE YOUR PRACTICE OF THE AFFIRMATIONS.

1. List one or more examples of actions you've taken recently that demonstrate each affirmation.

2. Identify the challenges that you met. The following questions will help:

    ◇ What risks did you take?
    ◇ Who may have been displeased by your decisions?
    ◇ Which of your actions required the most courage and why?

3. List the benefits that resulted for you and others, and describe how these benefits add to the amount of love in your life.

✦ ◇ ✦ **ACTION STEPS** ✦ ◇ ✦
COUPLES

1. Describe for each other specific examples when your partner's actions demonstrated one or more of the affirmations.

2. Identify the benefits that resulted for you both, and perhaps for others as well.

3. Look for additional examples in your partner's actions during the coming days and weeks, bring them to your partner's attention, and express your gratitude.

9

Men Can Be Heroes!

✦ ✧ ✦

If the power of love is to replace the power of domination, and if the code that supports male entitlement will be transformed into affirmations that support equality for all, then we men must make it happen. This can be our shining moment, and each of us has a role to play. In order to become part of the solution, we must be willing to evaluate and change our patterns of behavior and *help other men do the same.* Learning the traditional male code was not a solitary endeavor. It took years of indoctrination and continuous reinforcement by just about every person we encountered. This chapter opens a discussion on how we can help one another resist the tide of social forces that continues to promote the status quo. I'll describe men who are doing their part and offer suggestions on how you can join them.

One of my female clients shared the following example. Her story beautifully represents one of the many moments that happen every day of a man's life, moments when he faces a decision regarding whether to support the traditional male code or the code of affirmations instead. As you read the story, ask yourself what you would do if you found yourself in the same situation.

Joanna is a forty-two-year-old single woman from a fairly traditional Italian-American family. "I was the only daughter in the family and both my two brothers and my parents figured I'd leave home only when I either got married or died," she explained. She broke with that expectation during her early twenties when she purchased and moved into a small condominium in the town where she grew up. Her parents and brothers were outspoken in their belief that this was a mistake, but their chorus of nay saying eventually faded.

Four months ago Joanna made a second move. This time she purchased a home in a community twenty-five minutes away by car from her parents and brothers. Joanna's second move reignited all the old judgments from her family about her ability to take care of herself in the world as a single woman. "My brother, Pat, feels like he's helping me by badgering me to sell the house. He tells me it's too big for me and way too much for me to handle." Joanna went on to describe how she explained to Pat that his negativity insulted her and did not support her. "I call him sometimes to ask for his opinion on things because he's got more experience than I do as a homeowner, but I'm not looking for him to tell me how to do anything or make any decisions for me. I'd just like him to share his ideas."

During the extraordinarily rainy summer Joanna's area experienced recently, one cinderblock wall in her new home's foundation began seeping water into the basement. Joanna called a landscape architect. She asked Pat to be with her during the consultation, expecting that Pat's male presence would assure a respectful demeanor from the architect, a man Joanna had never met.

Shortly after the architect arrived, it became clear to Joanna that he was a man who respected women. He directed all of his questions and comments to her, despite Pat's presence. This impressed Joanna, as she'd endured many experiences in which male professionals who were supposedly interacting with her consistently addressed her male companion instead. This occurred, for example, when Joanna last shopped for a new car and brought along her friend, Jack. The salesmen at each dealership directed their comments to Jack despite Joanna's clear indication that she, and not Jack, wanted to buy.

As the architect explained the options for fixing the water problem, Pat interrupted him. Glaring at Joanna, Pat blurted out, "This house is just too much for you—you never would have had this problem if you'd been sensible and stayed in your apartment—what do you need this big house for anyway?!"

There followed a tense moment while Joanna considered how best to respond. The landscape architect scratched his beard and nodded his head while looking down. Then he broke the silence. Looking Pat squarely in the eye he said, "I don't get what you just said to your sister—I have two younger sisters and two younger brothers and I feel like it's really important for me to support them instead of tear them down. What's your big problem about your sister having this house? So the house has a problem with the grading next to this wall—problems come along with every house and you just get the problem fixed, right? Why don't you talk to her in a way that helps her decide the best way to fix the problem instead of putting her down? Isn't that what family and friends are supposed to do for one another?"

Instead of saying nothing, as most people may have done, this man took the risk of asking Pat to reconsider his use of male entitlement and power as domination. He challenged Pat to act in a loving manner toward his sister. The architect decided to use his power as a man to hold another man accountable for his offensive behavior. In doing so, he gave a gift to Pat and Joanna. It was a courageous thing to do.

Joanna remembered feeling stunned and tears coming to her

eyes. "I'd never had a man stick up for me like that," she said, beginning to tear up all over again as she told the story. "That was such a great thing to do—and he didn't even know me!" She went on to describe how Pat looked at the man for a few seconds and then walked a few steps away, keeping his eyes downcast. "He was quiet for the rest of the time the landscape guy was there. But you know what? Pat hasn't put me down once in the two weeks since then! I know it had to do with what that guy said because the change was immediate. He didn't even know him, but just having another man tell him that what he was doing was wrong and pointing him in a better direction seemed to make an incredible impact. Pat even followed his direction and gave me some good advice about which way I should go with fixing the water problem in my basement."

"What that man said to Pat was the best kind of support," Joanna continued, "the kind of thing real friends do for one another—you know, set each other straight by telling the truth instead of just going along with what the other guy's saying. That takes courage."

A realist, Joanna knew that the change in her brother was likely to be short-lived. She decided that when Pat started questioning her ability to manage the house again, she'd refer him back to what this man told him. "While I'm grateful to the landscape contractor, the whole thing also makes me angry. After all, where do you men get off deciding that you don't have to treat us like equals and take us seriously? Why did it take another man to get Pat to treat me with common courtesy and respect?"

Pat heard something from the landscape architect that he had refused to hear from his sister. As Joanna realized, however, this shift was likely to be short-lived. In most men's everyday worlds, such corrective encounters among men are rare. Joanna realized that support for such a change would need to be persistent in order to have a chance at shifting Pat's pattern of behavior.

I'm reminded of the laughable, and at times tragic, drama that too frequently unfolds within courtroom domestic violence cases. Self-inflated judges use their bully pulpits to lecture, cajole, encourage, and instruct men who have beaten their wives to "stop that right now" and "start treating her right," hoping perhaps that the authority of their office will sear the words into men's heart, thus changing his behavior as he moves forward in life. The same judges go on to release these men without mandating them into a batterers' intervention program that could potentially save their lives and the lives of their family members. Perhaps they tell themselves that such a mandate is unnecessary or too significant an infringement upon the man's freedom. Released back into a world that in no way provides guidance on how to enact the judge's directive, but rather affirms the man's domination of his partner, the men almost invariably resume their crimes.

After seeing this drama repeated time and again, I'm come to believe that what I'm witnessing is a failure of courage on the part of certain judges. They use power as domination to berate the men in court, putting on a show of "doing the right thing"; however, they don't follow through and mandate them into the right kind of intervention because they know that doing so brings political risk. Men of the middle and upper classes are very powerful, and many judges do not have the will to hold them accountable for crimes against women and children. They fear the backlash that may accompany such action. The so-called "father's rights" movement, which musters groups of men to protest what they see as unjust custody and divorce decisions, exemplifies what the judges fear should they decide to prioritize women's safety over men's entitlement.

In addition to a failure of courage, the decision to refrain from using one's power to hold a man accountable for his use of male entitlement, whether or not that use of entitlement rises to the level of abuse, is a failure of love. Love is not blind support. It's having the courage to tell the truth and use one's power to do what's right for everybody concerned.

We men face the challenge to create connections with one another where there are neither one-time admonishments nor the usual promotions for the traditional male code, but something new. That something new is a self- and collective examination that holds us accountable for the negative things we do to others, helps us make reparations and be respectful and loving, and guides us to attend to our shared human interests. Men are building such initiatives, and sometimes in the most unlikely of places.

Daniel, a Korean-American man who works as a supervisor within a major U.S. corporation, came to see me for a consultation because of increasing exhaustion, which contributed to growing isolation from his wife, Amy, also Korean-American, and a doctoral student at a prestigious university. Daniel's work team had endured repeated downsizings during the previous three years but no corresponding decrease in workload. Consequently, he and all the members of his staff were routinely working fourteen-hour days. His team's morale had reached an all-time low and two of his staff members were "out on stress disabilities." Recently, he began picking up signs from his management suggesting that his own job was likely to be among those cut in the next reorganization.

Therapy included Daniel's introduction to George, a man who had faced many of the same challenges within his own workplace and had started a weekly discussion group for downsizing survivors. George, along with the other members of the group, became Daniel's mentor and friend. George had decided two years ago to begin prioritizing connections with family and friends over the ever-increasing demands of the corporate workplace. He assembled the discussion group for mutual support and guidance. The group encouraged Daniel to take time off from work to be with Amy (Daniel had a stockpile of vacation days but was frightened that using them would flag him for downsizing). The men in the group also encouraged him to begin setting limits on the number of assignments he accepted from his manager. In these and other ways, they helped Daniel begin resisting the traditional male code in favor of the affirmations described in Chapter Eight.

At first, Daniel thought these actions would seal his selection for termination, so he updated his resume and began refreshing his network of business contacts. He began identifying and exploring career change options. He also worked closely with Amy to create a budget and financial plan that provided them maximum economic security. Feeling empowered by these actions, as well as by his growing perspective on the unreasonable expectations from his employer, he eventually went well beyond the suggestions offered by the men in the group. He began leaving work promptly at 5:00 PM every day and strongly encouraged those reporting to him to do the same. He sliced his team's workload nearly in half by saying no to a great many assignments. He began spending more time and energy planning and following through with family activities. His expanding group of friends set about having monthly dinners to celebrate the achievements each member and his or her partner were making in taking their lives back from corporate America and reinvesting in their most important relationships.

Within six months, Daniel and Amy were enjoying major changes in their lives. Instead of feeling isolated and depressed, as they had at the start of therapy, they now felt a strong connection to each other as well as to their expanding community of friends. The question the couple raised during their intake session regarding the likely need for anti-depressant medication was never mentioned again.

Surprisingly, Daniel was not downsized. His staff members were noted to be performing more effectively than ever before, their strong morale making them the envy of the department. Daniel recently reported, "My manager now refers to me as her 'Work/Life Guru' and has invited me to share my strategies with all her teams."

The discussion group initiated by George is one example of a growing number of grassroots community efforts that help men support one another in examining and shifting the values that drive their lives, families, and society as a whole. NOMAS, the National Organization for Men Against Sexism, is one example of a longstanding broad-based organization with these kinds of goals. NOMAS is committed to creating a world that affirms equality for people of all genders, races, and sexual orientations. Becoming active in such an organization or starting a group of your own is a great way to work toward making positive change happen.

One way to start is by organizing a reading and discussion group among male friends. Nathan McCall's books *Makes Me Wanna Holler: A Young Black Man in America* and *What's Going On,* as well as *Men's Work: How to Stop the Violence That Tears Our Lives Apart* and all the other books by Paul Kivel, are great starting places. Anything written by bell hooks, Alice Walker, or Arundhati Roy is an excellent addition. John Stoltenberg's *Refusing to be a Man* and Leslie Feinberg's *Trans Liberation: Beyond Pink or Blue* are other must-reads.

It is important for each man to recognize that, like it or not, we are role models for the men and boys around us. Through our actions and words, we influence the path that males as a group follow—we continually model what it means to be a man. There is little neutral ground. Either we approach our daily lives and relationships in a manner that is supportive of the traditional male code and the male entitlement it promotes, or we find the courage to embrace the code of affirmations instead. The choice is ours to make. The rewards, as well as the consequences, are many, far-reaching, and have great impact upon our own lives, as well as the lives of our loved ones and communities.

The work of changing our attitudes and choices presents an ongoing series of challenges. Chapter Ten provides ideas and suggestions for approaching the challenges of creating change.

✦ ✧ ✦ ACTION STEPS ✦ ✧ ✦
MEN

1. This chapter portrays male heroism as the courage to stand up for fairness, mutual respect, and love as guiding principles within everyday life—the values that social activist heroes Mohandas Gandhi, Martin Luther King Jr., and Cesar Chavez brought to the world stage. I challenge you to identify at least three specific actions you can take within your partnership, as a parent, or within another significant relationship during the next week that demonstrate your commitment to fairness, mutual respect, and love.

2. Discuss your plans with at least one other man.

3. Follow through with your planned actions and note the resulting benefits. Continue to seek new ways to enact your commitment to fairness, mutual respect, and love.

✦ ✧ ✦　**ACTION STEPS**　✦ ✧ ✦
WOMEN

1. Mainstream female heroes Betsy Ross and Mother Teresa typify the "heroic" supporting roles that patriarchy assigns women. Betsy Ross embroidered the flag, but she wasn't invited to sign the Declaration of Independence. Mother Teresa cared for the destitute, but she didn't help them organize to demand adequate shelter and healthcare. Identify at least two sheroes, women whose revolutionary work increased the fairness, mutual respect, and love experienced by those treated unfairly. Fannie Lou Hamer, Audre Lorde, Urvashi Vaid, and Emma Goldman serve as examples. List five attributes that characterize these women.

2. Using the five attributes that you identified as a guide, list two actions that you can take during the next week within your partnership, as a parent, or within another significant relationship that will increase the fairness, mutual respect, and love that you and others experience.

3. Follow through with those actions and note the resulting benefits.

✦ ✧ ✦　**ACTION STEPS**　✦ ✧ ✦
COUPLES

1. Heroism within intimate partnerships often comes in the form of acts of caring both small and large. Recall something your partner did to nurture your relationship. Maybe you received a simple "I love you" email when you arrived at the office one morning and it made your day. Perhaps

your partner went all out one Saturday morning and served you an elaborate breakfast in bed. Or it could be that, like the examples in this chapter, your partner stood up for you during a family discussion, or makes certain to prioritize your life together over the demands of his or her work.

2. Share with each other at least three of these recollections, describing how these actions enrich your life and your connection to each other.

3. Listen carefully to each other and make notes if that will help you remember. Make a commitment to performing similar actions during the days and weeks ahead.

10

Creating Lasting Change

✦ ✧ ✦

"Just do it!" the slogan says—and for once, though I rarely see anything of value in advertising, I'm inclined to agree. Sticking with a course of change proves difficult, however, and the question for some may be, "Just do what?" This chapter offers suggestions for staying on course. Some of these recommendations are new, and others, introduced within previous chapters, are re-emphasized and further developed here. The essence of change, like the essence of love, is action. So use what I give you to spark further thought, discussion, and, most of all, action.

Suggestions for creating lasting change:

- ✦ Define your goals clearly.
- ✦ Recognize that creating change requires *doing things differently.*
- ✦ Accept that conflict is a normal part of relationships.
- ✦ Continuously develop your critical consciousness.
- ✦ Keep your eye on the balance of power.

+ Put time and energy into friendships.
+ Seek professional help- but don't follow anybody's advice blindly.
+ Work for social justice.

DEFINE YOUR GOALS CLEARLY

Clearly defined goals keep you on track and provide your measures for success—and if your goals are not clearly defined you will have no way to gauge whether or not they've been achieved. This may sound incredibly obvious and simplistic, but many people who desperately want change in their couple partnership cannot readily describe precisely what the change should look like.

I advise my clients to visualize achievement of each goal as though they're watching the videotape of themselves engaged in the action that marks success. I ask them to describe what they see themselves doing.

Your goals will undoubtedly evolve as you achieve some of them and refine others. Always strive to keep them clear and specifically stated. Below are examples of goals for couples:

+ Both of us will know our son's schedule of activities, be acquainted with his friends' parents, make ourselves equally available to take him where he needs to go, and stay aware of how he's doing at school.
+ We will each report that we feel listened to and cared about by the other.
+ We will encourage one another to nurture our friendships. We will do this by equitably sharing family responsibilities (housework, childcare, eldercare) so that each of us gains access to one free evening every week.

Whenever you become unclear about your objectives, talk your thoughts and feelings over with others whom you trust. Clearly envisioning your destination makes it much easier to stay on track.

RECOGNIZE THAT CREATING CHANGE REQUIRES *DOING THINGS DIFFERENTLY*

You can think and talk until you're exhausted and nothing about your relationship with a partner, friend, family member, or coworker is likely to change unless you commit to action. This point may be self-evident to many readers, but I emphasize this simple idea because talking passes too frequently for change or a necessary prelude to change (when it is in reality often a never-ending preliminary step).

Confusion on this point is sometimes greatest for those who have been in certain types of individual psychotherapy. Many therapists and counselors, steeped in theories about insight and communication, exacerbate their clients' dilemmas by promoting the notion that talking about a concern equals doing something about it.

It is following through on one's commitment to action that creates change, allowing new patterns of experience to unfold. When this transformation disrupts the previously established predictability of relationships (and in many cases also the previously established dynamics of power), it is important to brace for encounters that undermine your commitment to the new course. When we start doing things differently, whether the difference is welcome, unwelcome, planned, unplanned, agreed upon, or not, we usually encounter some emotional discomfort, often feelings of loss and uncertainty. Invariably, we upset others, and they try to get us to reverse the change. These are normal, predictable, and manageable aspects of the process.

If we want things to turn out differently, we must *do* things differently. It really boils down to this fact. So read this and other books for information and inspiration, talk about your concerns with your partner, and surround yourself with people you love and respect who will give you honest feedback as well as the kind of support that includes expectations of follow-through and accountability; but expect things to change only when you start doing things differently!

ACCEPT THAT CONFLICT IS A NORMAL PART OF RELATIONSHIPS

Several years ago, I interviewed a married couple who were clients of a psychiatrist colleague, and afterwards, I strongly recommended family therapy. These were people who needed to sit in the same room with each other and receive coaching by a therapist or team of therapists on how to do things differently. They were a white, middle-class family: a man, his wife, and their two teenaged sons, both of whom were well on their way toward delinquency. The sons' behavior confused and frightened the parents who were often at odds with one another on how to respond. When the police escorted their fifteen-year-old home during the wee hours one morning because of his drunk and disorderly behavior, the parents were unable to agree on a plan of action. As a result, they gave the boy no consequences or additional structure in response to this crisis. A short time after this incident, the father, diagnosed by his psychiatrist with clinical depression and an anxiety disorder, entered an inpatient psychiatric ward.

I worked as a clinician on the ward and that's where I had the opportunity to meet with the couple. I advised them, as well as their psychiatrist, that family therapy, starting with the parents, would empower them to do such essential and fundamental things as set up enforceable house rules and other reasonable expectations for their sons. The good doctor thanked me for my recommendation, noting that he was in agreement with my assessment. He added, however, that in his opinion each family member's personal issues (he identified "conflict avoidance" as chief among each of the parents' issues) signified the need for at least another year of individual therapy before they'd be ready to face one another in couple or family therapy.

Each of the four family members had already been meeting weekly with separate staff therapists at the psychiatrist's practice for the better part of two years. I wondered what the psychiatrist could possibly mean. After all, these people lived together in the same house, two of them actually sleeping together in the same bed! I had to assume that all four bumped into each other now and then, maybe even ate together on occasion, yet in his opinion they needed another year of secret weekly talks with outsiders before dealing with one another face-to-face. The father's despair had landed him in a psychiatric hospital, and the family was falling apart despite each member's dutiful compliance with the prescription that they spend one hour each week talking with their respective therapists. If conflict avoidance was a problem for these parents, the professional help that the family received was only exacerbating that problem. The treatment team at the hospital, me included, could not convince the psychiatrist to change his approach, and we could not convince the family to contract with a different treating professional. It was not within our power to disconnect this family from the "help" they were receiving.

This couple (and their psychiatrist) badly needed reassurance that conflict in and of itself is not a bad thing. On the contrary, it's a normal part of all relationships. Conflict marks the occurrence of a difference in perspective, understanding, preference, or experience. Monica McGoldrick, one of my family therapy mentors, tells the story of her first interview with one couple. She listened to one partner say, "I have no reference point for this, my parents never experienced even a momentary disagreement as far as I can tell—they were always totally in sync with one another." Reflecting on this comment, Monica says, "I listened to this guy and thought, how sad if that's true—it's more likely they were just really good at keeping disagreements out of the children's sight—because if that were true it would mean his parents never even got close to one another." She continued, "No two people can really get to know one another without getting into disagreements and conflicts about some things; even identical twins don't share exactly the same ideas on everything!"

The willingness to respectfully identify and address conflicts, therefore, is an essential life skill that applies to every one of our relationships. Conflict resolution at best proceeds through a discussion of differences, a shared effort to identify potential solutions that might equitably satisfy the needs of all concerned, and, finally, a shared commitment to follow through on the mutually agreed-upon course of action. When a discussion of differences is not possible because one partner refuses to participate, the remaining partner needs to take this dismissal into account; nevertheless, they need to launch forward into action anyway, not allowing their partner to squelch their ability to create change.

CONTINUOUSLY DEVELOP YOUR CRITICAL CONSCIOUSNESS

Critical consciousness means evaluating what goes on in the world. This requires a keen awareness of the motivations and power dynamics operating behind the scenes. I've discussed the importance of critical consciousness for recognizing the traditional male code and male entitlement as social conventions instead of facts of nature. It is important to expand your application of critical consciousness to all aspects of life in our society. The more we work on developing critical consciousness the more clearly we see what's really happening within all the social systems that we participate in, including families and intimate partnerships. As critical consciousness expands, so does our realization of the possibilities for constructive change.

Apply critical consciousness to the sources of the information you receive on a daily basis. Carefully consider whose interests are shaping that information.

We live in a world where misinformation from many sources attempts to take from us much that is of value, including our time, energy, self-respect, self-love, and creativity. We find ourselves continually bombarded by television, radio, newspaper, magazine, and internet advertising asking us to buy a myriad of things, each guaranteed to improve our lives and make ourselves and those around us happier. For many people the result of this non-stop sales pitching is, predictably (and profitably), a belief in their own inadequacy, negativity and hopelessness about their life circumstances, and a belief that buying things will make life better. I recently heard a radio commercial claim, "It takes the right product to get great abs!" Funny, I thought it took regular exercise and proper diet! What was I thinking?

Many outstanding volumes have been written about the ways that marketing, public relations, and government systems try to dupe us into believing untruths that will lead us to believe and act in ways that have negative consequences for us, those around us, and the natural world. I strongly encourage you to read the work of authors Naomi Klein, Winona Laduke, Ralph Nader, Noam Chomsky, Alice Walker, Pearl Cleage, Arundhati Roy, Greg Palast and John Pilger. In addition to reading these authors, below are three activities you can start doing today that will help you critically evaluate everyday sources of information by nurturing your mind, spirit, and body:

1. Listen to public access radio and television, media that have *no* corporate sponsorship, instead of (or at least in addition to) the advertising-based programming of the mainstream media outlets. WBAI Pacifica Radio out of New York City (available also at wbai.org) is one example. The more you listen to non-corporate sponsored media, the more you will be immersed in information that prioritizes human values over the profit motive.

2. If you participate in a religious community, consider the following questions and talk them over with your religious leaders:

   + Does my religious community teach that all people, across differences of faith, gender, skin color, sexual orientation, ethnicity, socioeconomic class, and all other dimensions of diversity are equally human and therefore due the same consideration and rights?
   + Does my religious community affirm or disavow the use of violence as a means for solving problems?

3. Treat your body with reverence. Smoke, or eat junk food, and you are allowing your health to be sacrificed for the profits of the Philip Morris and Coca Cola corporations. Nurture your relationship with your body by making sure to do all the basics that

are crucial to healthful resilience: eat a nutritious diet, get enough sleep, and exercise, stretch, and/or meditate regularly.

As these activities illustrate, exercising critical consciousness and working to prevent yourself, and others, from being exploited reinforces the value you place on love and respect.

KEEP YOUR EYE ON THE BALANCE OF POWER

Whether you are in a long-term committed partnership, in a dating relationship, or just thinking about asking someone special out for the very first time, I advise you to pay close attention to the balance of power between the two of you. If you imagine an intimate relationship to be a house, the balance of power within the relationship is the house's foundation. The more solid and level the foundation, the stronger will be the house—relationship—that is built upon it.

As has been described within previous chapters, there are power implications connected to just about every identity characteristic you can name: age, gender, skin color, ethnicity, sexual orientation (and the degree to which one is "out" if gay, lesbian, or bisexual), social class background and family connections, the amount of money we have, educational background, language skills, immigration status, height, weight, body type, the degree to which our appearance fits mainstream standards of beauty, and the state of our health. In every relationship we have with another person these identity characteristics, theirs and ours, contribute to the balance of power between us. I encourage you to pay attention to this power equation and strive to find ways to create equality.

If you live with your partner, this means taking a look at the ways differences of opinion are resolved, how money and expenses are managed, and the ways in which all other aspects of decision making that affect the lives of household participants are approached. For example, do both partners, as well as other household members (children and extended family who may be residing with you), consistently feel that it's safe to acknowledge differences of feeling or opinion? Are all feelings consistently expressed by both partners in a manner that is non-threatening? Does each partner feel listened to? Does each partner feel they have complete control over when and in what manner they engage in sexual activity? Is "no" always respected?

If there is a disparity in income, or if one partner works outside the home while the other does not, what is done to make certain that both partners have a fair share in the ownership of assets and authority when it comes to making spending decisions? Does each partner shoulder an equal or equivalent share in the mundane tasks of home management, such as doing the laundry from start to finish (including folding, ironing, and stowing), food shopping (including paying attention to inventory so you know when shopping is necessary and what needs to be purchased), cooking, and scrubbing the floors and toilets? If there are children involved, do both partners share equally in their care—including things like diaper-changing and bathing, scheduling planning (including arranging for childcare, play dates, and other activities, as well as arranging for transportation as necessary), helping with homework, keeping track of when medical and dental check-ups are needed, and paying attention to the children's needs for clothing, medicine, and other supplies as well as shopping for these staples? In a same-sex relationship, does each partner feel respected, supported, and protected by the other when it comes to their decisions regarding their pattern of "outness?" The answers to these questions provide keys to understanding the balance of power within a committed domestic partnership, and, more important still, the kinds of changes that should be enacted.

Within dating relationships, differences like gender, skin color, and many socioeconomic class indicators are obvious, but because both parties know relatively little about one another, and are usually determined to be on their best behavior during the earliest stages of courtship, it can be difficult to evaluate the degree to which one's dating partner is interested in developing an equal relationship. It may be fairly easy to determine if an individual adheres to the traditional male code, as well as their participation in racism, sexism, and homophobia, by paying close attention to the ways they treat others who are similar to and different from themselves. These patterns provide an indication of the extent to which a person either agrees with or resists the power imbalances supported by society's mainstream.

Many points from the paragraphs above regarding committed partnerships also apply to dating relationships, notably including the ways that each person deals with differences of opinion or feeling. For example, do both dating partners acknowledge differences thoughtfully and respectfully, welcoming an open discussion and compromise, or does one or both seek to avoid confronting points of difference? Do one or both partners behave in a controlling fashion such that the only opinion that seems to register is their own? Early signs of overly controlling behavior include a pattern in which one partner seems to be happy only when he or she is the one to choose the activity, location, time frame, or other aspects of time spent together; consistently insists upon paying the bill; shows an unwelcome degree of interest in how the other person spends their time when the two are apart; and disrespects "no" as an answer by consistently pushing their agenda.

Once you've taken a good hard look at the power differences, it's time to begin enacting changes that will make things fairer. Note that I said enact rather than discuss. While it may be useful to collect data (one friend of mine got himself and his partner pedometers so they could log the hours each spent chasing and caring for their toddler during the evening hours) and negotiate, change requires action.

Action that makes committed partnerships fairer can take many forms, including the creation of a schedule in which all aspects of the food shopping, cooking, housecleaning, laundry service, bill paying, and pet care are divided in an agreed-upon manner. It is important for these kinds of arrangements to be discussed both inside and outside the couple relationship, gathering input from trusted friends and family members. Those who have traditionally had less power within our society, including women, people of color, and people from less wealthy backgrounds, should be consulted and keenly listened to as the couple decides whether or not their planned division of family labor is equitable. People from more privileged backgrounds are generally less skilled at making these kinds of judgments as they are likely to overvalue the significance of any contributions by men beyond what has traditionally been obliged. In other words, men whose background has taught them to expect to be serviced by a wife may at first believe that vacuuming the living room rug or loading the dishwasher now and then constitutes splitting the housework.

When it comes to money, some partners find that it's important to establish separate financial accounts in order to equalize their power, with each paying for joint expenses at a rate proportional to their relative incomes. For example, if one earns twice as much as the other, then the former contributes twice as much to shared expenses. In relationships where one partner takes care of home and childcare responsibilities instead of pursuing paid employment, it makes sense for the other to give them one half of their income.

Patterns of sexual behavior reflect the power dynamics within a relationship. For example, it is revealing to explore where responsibility for birth control lies. If the woman partner takes sole responsibility, then a change may well be in order to make things fairer. Also, when there is equity in the sexual component of a relationship, the answer from both partners will always be "no" to the question: "Do you ever engage in sexual activity at a time or in a manner that you are not entirely comfortable with?"

Within dating relationships, it is reasonable to expect shared responsibility and authority. Each partner contributes equally to decisions about their relationship—how much time will be spent together; where they'll go; what activities will be engaged in and who else might be invited; how expenses will be divided; and if, when, and in what ways they will be sexually intimate.

When words fail to register so agreements on change cannot be reached (as was discussed in Chapter Three), we are challenged to forge ahead and make what we believe are necessary changes anyway. Thus, it may be evident to a woman that she alone does the laundry, cooking, and cleaning, while her partner contributes nothing that counterbalances this inequity. If her partner, furthermore, will not engage in a productive discussion when she raises the issue of this inequity, then unilateral change remains her only reasonable option aside from acquiescence. She might begin doing only her own laundry and cooking, leaving him to fend for himself in these areas. As was discussed within Chapter Three, structural change such as this is the only thing that some partners, too frequently men, seem able to "hear."

PUT TIME AND ENERGY INTO FRIENDSHIPS

Despite what many of us have been led to believe, nobody and no couple can do it all alone. The primary messages delivered by the most influential institutions of our society, including the major media and most of our workplaces, would have us believe that the little time remaining after we fulfill the ever-increasing demands of employment should be spent watching television and purchasing the consumer goods it promotes. Intimate partnerships and family relationships are portrayed as important reasons to buy things (like makeup, plastic surgery, diet programs, self-help books, clothes, toys, cleaning agents, fabric softener, and minivans) rather than as the centerpiece of a meaningful and fulfilling life. These basic human connections are sometimes acknowledged within corporate workplaces with a grudging nod to "work/life balance." Within this world view, little attention is given to friendships, recreation, and other vital aspects of life.

The traditional male code supports the problem by teaching men that relationship work is women's work, life's priority is paid employment, self-reliance is more important than collaboration, and aggression is a reasonable way to resolve conflicts. The code also teaches that "real men" limit their willingness to express feelings, strive for dominance rather than intimacy, and don't get emotionally close to other men. All of this works against men's ability to establish and maintain friendships.

Maintaining a network of loving friends makes an important contribution to your health, sanity, and the resilience of a strong relationship with an intimate partner, if you currently have one. This may seem counter-intuitive in the face of the relentless barrage of hype we face about the necessity for every adult to be partnered, as well as the mythology teaching us to believe that a good partnership fulfills every relational need, but the fact of the matter is, a web of friendships provides the most durable, reliable, and empowering means for meeting our human needs for connection and support over the long haul. Friendship networks also provide the support that helps make intimate partnerships strong. So it's not an either/or proposition when it comes to friends and intimate partnerships, and you should run, not walk, away from any potential partner who suggests otherwise.

It may be useful to imagine a group of friends as a community that enriches our life-long journey. Friends help us create and understand our experiences. They propel us forward through adulthood with confidence, helping us make sense of our evolving paths and live up to our highest values. After all, true friends are not those who offer unconditional affirmation for everything that we do, but rather people who love and respect us enough to risk letting us know when they're concerned that we may not be acting in our own best interest or in that of family members. Our most helpful friends, in other words, are those who support us as we try to live the affirmations described within Chapter Eight

Having a network of friends who you can count on to accompany you through good times and bad is vitally important. If you enjoy such friendships, then you are already doing one of the most important things you can to support your emotional health as well as the health of your family relationships and your intimate partnership, if you are involved in one. If you do not have such a network, working to build friendships of this sort should be a top priority.

SEEK PROFESSIONAL HELP, BUT DON'T FOLLOW ANYBODY'S ADVICE BLINDLY

One of our most important life skills is the willingness to ask for and benefit from help when we need it. Far from signifying weakness, and contrary to what the traditional code might have us believe, *the strongest and most competent among us recognize that knowing when to seek assistance is a mark of great personal strength.* And make no mistake about it, many of the changes described in this book are difficult to enact—sometimes because they're not easy to conceptualize but more typically because it's emotionally stressful to challenge the status quo. A professional therapist, counselor, or coach can provide invaluable support as you plan, initiate, and weather the challenges that arise within any change of course. What you need to be ever mindful of, however, is that too many of these helping professionals, some unwittingly and some purposely, support the traditional male code and all the patterns of inequity it creates.

So while it's often a great idea to engage a therapist to help us change, it's also essential to carefully evaluate whether or not the therapist we choose is acting in our best interest. The opening page of Chapter Seven lists several ways that therapists and other helpers too frequently support the traditional male code. Use this list as a starting point for evaluating any therapist you are thinking about working with. Be an assertive customer by asking questions about their approach to helping, and question them further if you don't understand or agree with what they're saying or recommending. Therapy is an inexact science, so don't defer your own ideas, impulses, and judgments too readily. If you disagree with the therapist's recommendations, don't hesitate to seek a second opinion.

Discuss the therapist's recommendations with friends, particularly those friends who have developed a critical consciousness about how power and privilege operate and who support the affirmations in Chapter Eight. A few examples will make this point clearer. I consulted several years ago with a white middle-class heterosexual couple in which the woman felt as though her husband was abandoning her and the couple's two young children approximately three Saturdays of every month. He spent those Saturdays, and sometimes Sundays as well, adventuring with the members of his Harley Davidson motorcycle club. On the weekend days when the club did not have an excursion planned, the man spent time with the children. He didn't favor doing such things as feeding, bathing, and diapering, however, "because I have so little time with them I want to make sure it's quality time." His definition of quality time meant playtime.

When I asked him how it came to be that he spent so many weekends away from the family doing things that pleased him while his wife was virtually never provided with a similar opportunity to go off and do her own thing, he said (with a straight face, I might add), "She likes taking care of the kids—*that's* her thing!" She responded to this by angrily reciting a list of activities: going out to lunch and the movies with her girlfriends (many of whom she'd lost touch with), visiting museums, resuming her piano lessons, spending time reading, and working out at a nearby health club, that she had put aside more or less completely during the past five years, because she needed to take care of their kids and home during his weekend disappearances.

The husband experienced his wife's requests—that he share more of the responsibilities of childcare and spend less time away from home on the weekends so that she might be able to enjoy some respite (and maybe even recreation)—as attempts to "control" him. I mentioned my impression that he confused his wife's request for fairness with an effort to control him. "Don't take my word for it, though," I suggested, "discuss this with at least two women and two men whom you consider to have good sense about what fairness and control look like, and at our next meeting, let me know what they said." The next time we met, he reported that most of the people he had spoken with, both women and one of the men, had agreed with me. They had felt he had not been taking on his fair share of responsibilities and, furthermore, that he had needed to start giving his wife's time and interests the same degree of importance as he had given his own. "My friend, Bill, told me that I should wake up—he said, 'You need to figure out whether you want a partner or a maid because that woman you married didn't sign on to be your maid.'" The husband went on to report, "The only person who saw it the way I did was Larry, my friend from the motorcycle club, who told me, 'Anybody that'll begrudge a man his God-given freedom on a Saturday when it's perfect weather for riding has gotta be some kind of feminazi!'" After a couple of moments passed, the husband turned to his wife and said quietly, "You've got as much right to freedom as I do—it really *is* about being fair."

In another example, a therapist—after speaking with the woman's partner, siblings, parents, and children—advised her client that it would be a good idea for her to abstain from drinking alcoholic beverages for at least thirty days as the therapist believed alcohol was contributing to the tensions apparent in the client's relationship with each of these people, as well as causing her to miss time at work. Furious and feeling deeply insulted, the woman stormed out of the session. During the next several days, she told the story of what had happened with the therapist to three friends, and each of them found the courage to share their own concerns about the woman's abuse of alcohol. While she did not immediately accept the existence of her substance abuse problem and did not return to that therapist, years later after she had entered recovery, the woman described the therapist's comments and her subsequent discussions with friends as the period during which her system of denial began to unravel.

In a final example, Sandra, a thirty-five-year-old Chilean-American stay-at-home mother of four young children, had been told by her marriage counselor that she should work harder at keeping the children quiet during the evening, as well as at keeping the house cleaner, because Sandra's husband's depression and anxiety were exacerbated by the noise and lack of order within their home. Alex, Sandra's forty-two-year-old Uruguayan-American husband, who worked as a chemical engineer, stayed emotionally remote from Sandra and largely uninvolved with his children. He worked long hours and, upon returning home, liked to spend his evenings studying engineering journals. Saying that he'd been diagnosed as a child with what he called "anxious and depressive tendencies," it seemed to Sandra that Alex used this history to justify his isolation from the rest of the family.

Sandra talked over what was going on in therapy with some of her friends, and they told her to find a new therapist. One friend put it this way, " That counselor of yours has bought Alex's story hook, line, and sinker, and she wants you to pick up all his slack . . . you need someone who's going to look at what's going on from your perspective, too!" Taking her friends' advice to heart, Sandra insisted that the couple interview other therapists. Eventually they found a therapist who challenged Alex to join Sandra in the work of creating a relationship.

As these examples illustrate, it's a good idea to share a therapist's recommendations with your friends because they can help you test out the reasonableness of what's being suggested; doing so brings accountability, for both you and the therapist, to the therapeutic process. Friends can help you get to the bottom of why certain professional advice makes you feel uncomfortable. Is it that following the therapist's advice is likely to have destructive consequences for you and your family? Is your discomfort tied to the way those recommendations challenge your feelings of entitlement and control?

Loving friends can help you weather and make sense of the discomfort that inevitably accompanies even beneficial changes in your life and relationships. While it is often wise to seek professional help, it's also wise to check out what's being recommended with people you trust and respect.

WORK FOR SOCIAL JUSTICE

Working to advance social justice allows one's critical consciousness to rise to new levels. The more closely one examines daily life within America's mainstream the more evident it becomes that we have been accepting gross inequality as an entirely normal feature of daily life for a very long time. Waking up to this reality and working to change it can help us gain clarity about the inequality and power imbalances within our personal connections.

Consider the millions of people who work full-time for employers across the United States and other countries as well. Those of us who earn a living wage or better often seem to have little difficulty with the fact that a large number of full-time workers are paid less than a subsistence wage while a much smaller number receive millions of dollars yearly for their work. We are entirely accustomed to this enormous inequality, rarely if ever pausing to even notice, much less question, it. It's one of those things that many people accept as a fact of nature, like the fact that the sky is blue and the grass green.

In reality, however, this is a relatively new, accelerating, and far from universal phenomenon. Five hundred years ago, on this very continent, there were more than four hundred flourishing cultures, most of which would probably have appraised the kind of economic disparity which is normal to us today as inexplicable savagery. The concentration of enormous wealth within the hands of a very few and the corresponding impoverishment of a growing number of people was a far less pervasive reality prior to the INDUSTRIAL REVOLUTION. The trend accelerated at a furious rate during the 20th century, and continues today. This pattern is not universal, however. Many cultures across the world continue to value health, family, and community well-being over individual financial wealth.

As I draw attention to the economic inequality that many of us take for granted, you may find words like "socialist" and "communist" popping into your mind and wondering if these apply to me. I'll talk about why that happens later on. You may also find yourself almost reflexively conjuring rebuttals: "But people should be paid differently according to their level of responsibility, expertise, seniority, and personal investment!" Perhaps it makes sense for there to be some differential in earnings, but is it reasonable that people who work full-time are compensated so differently that some are unable to consistently afford shelter and food while others possess every conceivable luxury?

Our system of public education offers another example of *normalized inequality*. Some children attend school in modern buildings that offer the newest technology, including Internet access for every student, cutting-edge textbooks, and state-of-the-art athletic facilities. These schools may also offer the individualized attention that comes with classroom sizes limited to fifteen students. Children in other neighborhoods, on the other hand, attend school in leaky, broken-down buildings with inadequate heating and lighting, outdated textbooks, no athletic facilities, and classroom sizes topping fifty students. Many of us accept this inequality as though it were "natural."

Our system of health care provides a third example. Some families in our country enjoy insurance coverage that promises the very finest medical, mental health, and dental care. A large number of families, however, enjoy no such security. Again, many of us have come to accept this inequality.

One reason for our complacency is that the roots of inequality within our society have grown deep, strong, and validated by law. Europeans brought with them to this land a hierarchical system of wealth and property ownership that was the forebear of our current economic and political order. Within that system, hierarchies based upon class, gender, race, and sexual orientation were mandated by law.

Women were relegated to second-class citizenry. In fact, Western culture and its derivatives, former colonies such as the United States of America, have in many instances only recently recognized women as full citizens, worthy of voting rights and of holding property in their own names. For centuries, women were the legal wards of their fathers, and of their husbands upon marriage. Women in the United States were not allowed to vote until 1920, when the 19th amendment to the U.S. Constitution granted universal suffrage. Vestiges of women's second-class status still linger—unequal rates of pay for doing the same work as men (today it's $.73 for every dollar men earn doing the same job), continuing struggles over reproductive freedom, and uneven levels of protection offered survivors of domestic violence. Unfortunately, sexism thrives.

Similarly, institutionalized racism in the form of ethnic cleansing, or genocide, toward Native Americans, along with the enslavement of African-Americans, remains a legacy whose impact has yet to be fully acknowledged, much less resolved. Indeed, the legacy continues to be active. Many Native American communities continue to sue the government for restoration of property and land use rights guaranteed by treaty. The 1998 murder of James Byrd in Jasper, Texas, provides a horrifying demonstration of the current face of racism. Byrd, a disabled African-American man, was dragged to his death behind the pickup truck of his white assailants. African-Americans, as well as all other people of color, continue to struggle for equal protection, inclusion, and participation in virtually all aspects of the life of our society.

Finally, consider the different experiences of the following two couples. Tasha and Said, both Syrian-American, decided to marry after dating for a year. They were both sixty years old and had outlived their first marriage partners. They set the date and had a beautiful ceremony at their church, followed by a great celebration with their family and friends. The state's recognition of their legal marriage bond affords them a host of benefits, including inheritance guarantees and access to healthcare benefits from one another's employers. Another couple, George and

Steven, after dating for a year, decided to have a commitment ceremony and began living together. They set a date and had a beautiful ceremony at their church, followed by a great celebration with their families and friends. The state would not grant them a marriage license, however. All the benefits that official recognition of their marriage grants Tasha and Said were withheld from George and Steven. Again, many people never question this inequality. Indeed, some people argue that George and Steven's desire for the same benefits the state provides Tasha and Said is an attempt to gain "special rights." The right to equal protection under federal law, which has been extended to women, the disabled, and people of color, has not yet been granted to gay, lesbian, bisexual, and transgender people.

When compared to these examples, the inequalities of power between many men and women within couple relationships, and their acceptance, fall right into line. Many couples, as well as their friends, family members, and helping professionals, don't acknowledge, explore, and challenge inequality and misuse of power because such things are accepted as normal, perhaps even natural and unchangeable. Moreover, we face powerful disincentives for even identifying these issues. As I mentioned earlier, just thinking or reading about inequality can bring to mind all sorts of nasty labels: "liberal," "bleeding heart," "un-American," "socialist," "communist," "male basher," and "whistle-blower" to name but a few. Publicly calling attention to inequality often brings down a storm of such words upon us, and can lead to ostracism, job loss, and even physical assault.

Why does this happen? Why this knee-jerk, negative response to looking at inequality? Let's take a look at whose interests are served. As long as white people are preoccupied with their fear that the growing equality of people of color will cause them to lose something, men are preoccupied with keeping women in line, and heterosexual people are preoccupied with "defending marriage," these groups are very unlikely to recognize their common interest in holding the executives at Halliburton, Enron, Tyco, and WorldCom accountable for their thievery, destruction of jobs, and offenses against the environment we all share. Preventing the majority of people from taking a critical look at inequality serves the interests of those most powerful by maintaining the status quo. It helps us keep buying the idea that inequality is somehow in our best interests. The reality is exactly the opposite.

What does living in a world that teaches us to support inequality mean to our quest for love within personal relationships? If we understand love as a way of relating in which honesty, vulnerability, generosity, care-giving, respect, and affection are practiced for the benefit of both partners, then fairness is the platform on which this exchange must take place. Or, as bell hooks writes, "There can be no love without justice." *Living in a world that devalues fairness makes it difficult to strive for love.*

Working to create more fairness in the world can fuel our commitment, and sharpen our vision for increasing the fairness within our intimate and family connections. For the most courageous, getting involved in social justice causes can be an important part of the effort to change our most important relationships.

With clear objectives in mind, a growing critical consciousness to shape your vision, and loving friends by your side, you can create the changes that will bring more love, happiness, and fairness to your most important relationships. Your journey of change offers the ongoing challenge of transforming deliberation into action. I wish you and your loved ones much energy and resolve as you rise to that challenge.

This book shines a spotlight on issues men often bring to intimate partnerships, as on well as the fundamental importance of power within relationships both personal and public. Chapter

Eleven, the book's final chapter, provides responses to questions that may have come to many readers' minds. I'm certain, however, that I will not address all of your questions—and that's not a bad thing. One of my primary goals is to inspire development of critical consciousness. At the heart of critical consciousness is a thirst for knowledge regarding how and why the social world operates as it does and what can be changed in order to increase fairness for everyone. If you finish reading the book and are left with more questions and the initiative to pursue answers, then I have done my job.

II

Dialogue

✦ ✧ ✦

The questions that follow reflect those that people ask when they initially encounter the ideas in this book. As you read each one, imagine how you would answer it before reading my response. Evaluate both the similarities and the differences, and you will gain the most from the dialogue.

Q. Are all men indoctrinated into the male code? Do some men have families, friends, or community connections that help them avoid buying into it?

A. Whether individual families reinforce or resist the code, the world overwhelms us with messages and modeling that promote it. Schools, community programs such as Little League and Boy Scouts of America, religious organizations, workplaces, and every type of informational and entertainment media participate. Messages reinforcing the code do not end in childhood, but persist as features of daily life within our communities. No man remains unaffected.

Resisting the male code first requires awareness, and then concerted effort that's best supported by a group of like-minded peers. Sexism, racism, and heterosexism, closely related to the male code, work pretty much the same way—if you don't pay attention to them, you unwittingly enact them.

I agree that a person's family and community background, along with their contemporary connections, affect *the extent* to which they buy into the code. The more actively a man tries to resist the code, particularly when supported by a group of friends, the more successfully he replaces the code with the affirmations described in Chapter Eight.

Bear in mind, however, that many social justice activists support the male code and other unfair realities. The civil rights movement of the 1950s and 1960s endorsed the male code even as it challenged racism. Movement leaders assigned women "second shift" rather than highly visible roles. Some civil rights leaders continue to spout anti-gay rhetoric. The contemporary women's movement often sidelines the needs of women of color and lesbians, and the gay rights movement has yet to significantly challenge its own sexism and racism. Take a look at most gay rights organizations and you'll find the people at the top "mostly male and mostly pale," as a friend of mine says. The patriarchal male code, racism, and homophobia exert such overwhelming influence that even people and organizations struggling for justice are not immune.

Q. Heterosexual men aren't the only ones who act entitled and abuse power. Some heterosexual women behave in the same ways as the worst male offenders, as do some gay men and lesbians in same-sex relationships. How do you account for that?

A. Absolutely true. This observation highlights the prime importance of "power as domination"—it's even more significant than gender.

Within heterosexual relationships, the man often holds more power due to his physical size and strength, access to money, professional status, and/or connections to powerful community members. Many men also firmly believe in their entitlement to authority. In this typical situation, the man may or may not misuse the power he holds.

In a small number of cases, the woman holds more power than her male partner due to her size and strength, access to money, professional status, and/or family and community connections. *Her* power advantage supersedes the usual expectation of male authority. Following the "power as domination" model, she may or may not choose to misuse the power she holds over her partner and other family members.

The same occurs in same-sex relationships. The presence of two male or two female partners does not assure equal power. With unfortunate regularity the partner who is physically stronger; has more money, connections, and professional status; and/or exudes more confidence because of being "out" and accepted by family and coworkers, chooses to misuse their advantage.

Power rarely aligns neatly, however. Men and women who hold the balance of physical, economic, and/or political power often discount their advantage. They argue that their partner's greater skill with language or larger network of friends matters more.

While almost everything we learn about how to be men and women conveys expectations of *male* dominance, the inclination to dominate can trump gender due to certain advantages (or when same-sex union makes gender moot). Patriarchy ordains very clear and simple rules. Chief among them: "Men should be in charge of everything" and "Use power to dominate." If circumstances defeat one of these rules, the other may still hold. If we embraced power as the responsibility to love, collaborate, and nurture, then we'd see a very different pattern. Intimate partners, regardless of gender, would handle their advantages with humility—striving to empower, support, and care for their significant others and children rather than dominate and control them.

Q. Are male entitlement, the male code, and power dynamics the only things that couples experiencing difficulties need to address in order to make things better?

A. Not at all. Instead, I argue that these matters must be acknowledged and addressed instead of ignored, which is what typically happens. Experience shows me that understanding a couple or family's conflicts requires evaluating power. Striving for equality and fairness promotes healing.

To help their clients, good counselors and therapists employ a variety of skills and techniques. They evaluate stressors across many life dimensions; construct a genogram (an extended family tree diagram) to explore multigenerational patterns; provide coaching on parenting, boundary marking, and other relational skills; and suggest involvement with community and self-help programs. They use dozens of other interventions as well. *Each and every one of these* should address male entitlement, the male code, and power imbalances.

Q. Lots of women go along with the male code wholeheartedly even though it devalues them. Why is that?

A. Women gain rewards for supporting the male code, but they risk severe consequences for challenging it. Thus women support the reprimand directed at boys to, "Stop acting like a girl!" (Rule #1) despite the implied scorn aimed at all females. Many women support Rule #2 ("Keep your feelings to yourself!") by enabling male partners, family members, and friends who are unwilling to express their emotions. They identify, express, and even resolve emotional dilemmas for their men. How many times have you heard a woman describe the time and energy she puts into keeping her husband and his sister, brother, or parents connected because he won't make an effort to talk with them directly? Women support Rule #3 ("Work is your first priority!") by sacrificing their own careers, friends, and community connections when their male partner's career calls for relocation. Each rule of the code casts supporting roles for girls and women.

Women across the world have long been forced to participate in this gendered drama, even when it's excruciatingly harmful to them. In accordance with Rule #7 ("Women are for sex!"), the practice of female genital mutilation "cleanses" women and prepares them for use by men. This practice, common to many traditional West African cultures, removes or mutilates the vulva and clitoris. In their book, *Warrior Marks: genital mutilation and the sexual blinding of women,* Alice Walker and Pratibha Parmar report that it is always women who perform genital mutilation upon girls.

While it may first seem outrageous that women inflict this violence upon other females, the logic becomes clear after further consideration. For within most cultures, including our own, women ensure that families follow tradition. They fill the role of "culture bearer." This assignment covers everything from planning celebrations for family birthdays, anniversaries, and holiday celebrations to making sure children and husbands dress properly before leaving home for the day. Women's acceptance of the culture bearing role frees men to pursue Rule #3 ("Work is your first priority!").

While I used female genital mutilation as an example because it emphasizes the extreme to which women must go to support male domination, it is important to recognize that most societies observe similarly violent traditions. Foot binding and female infanticide in China and veiling within some Islamic groups are examples. Corseting, cloistering of women during pregnancy, self-starvation, and plastic surgeries designed to meet impossible standards of beauty fall within the same category of traditions. They demonstrate America's enduring preoccupation with the domination, mutilation, and control of females. As these examples illustrate, traditions take many forms according to time, location, and fashion. Patriarchy—the father of the male code and all tradition—however, remains unchanged, solid as bedrock.

Many women play their assigned supporting role without complaint. "Good girls," beauty-fixated women, and self-effacing wives gain numerous rewards for their compliance. A few women succeed at turning the "power as domination" game to their advantage. They embody the male code themselves as a means to gain leadership posts within corporate, government, and other powerful institutions.

Penalties await girls and women who choose to resist. Here in the United States, they endure slurs like "tomboy," "man-hater," and "bitch." Heterosexual women who defer partnership, because the men they date burden rather than facilitate their lives, are made to feel like failures. In other parts of the world, women who resist genital mutilation or veiling invite ostracism, even death. Women who seek intimate partnerships with other women risk a similar fate.

Those who choose the course of resistance face many obstacles. It takes monumental courage to resign the role of culture bearer; it takes more courage still to assume the mantle of cultural reformer, one who demands and models equality. A number of excellent books have been written about aspects of this challenge, including Claudia Bepko and Jo-Ann Krestan's classic *Too Good for Her Own Good: Breaking Free From the Burden of Female Responsibility,* and, more recently, Susan Maushart's *Wifework.*

Harriet Lerner's classic bestsellers, including *The Dance of Anger* and *The Dance of Intimacy,* provide invaluable guidance as well.

Q. Can you please say more about critical consciousness? What is the alternative?

A. Introduced by Brazilian educator Paulo Freire, critical consciousness is a state of mind in which patterns of daily life are examined to reveal their underlying political and economic causes.

Critical consciousness frees us to make life-enhancing changes. For example, if a man believes that nature did not give him the ability to identify and share feelings, he behaves accordingly—stoicism, overuse of anger, and emotional distance help him dominate others. When he learns, however, that all human beings can express the full range of emotions, he faces a crossroads. Will he continue behaving in a manner that supports male supremacy, or will he begin to identify and share his feelings? Choosing the former continues his participation in a pattern of domination. Choosing the latter introduces emotional vulnerability, and the likelihood of greater intimacy with his partner and other people in his life—it offers the promise of love.

I call the alternative to critical consciousness "acquiescent consciousness." In this state of mind, individuals don't question power and don't challenge circumstances. They would not be disturbed by the George Orwell paraphrase, "Some people are more equal than others." Acquiescent consciousness is a state of resigned ignorance.

Q. There seems to be a political agenda in your work. Aren't therapists supposed to be objective and neutral?

A. All therapists follow a political agenda. Whether they recognize this fact, or admit to it, is another matter. A political agenda becomes more or less noticeable depending upon the extent to which it contrasts with society's most prominent political agenda. The more different your agenda is, the more obvious it becomes that you've got one. The political agenda of most therapists blends with the current mainstream.

How could it be otherwise when you think about the training most therapists receive? For example, during my undergraduate years at Cornell University and later, during my graduate studies at The City University of New York, I studied Freud, Jung, Erikson, Ellis, Beck, Bettelheim, Piaget, Masterson, and other white male luminaries from the field of psychology. The theories of these founding scholars overflow with prejudice against women, working- and poverty-class people, people of color, and gay, lesbian, bisexual, and transgender people.

Consequently, when most therapists begin practicing, they're thoroughly indoctrinated into a substantial collection of biases. More specifically, they believe that thinking should always take precedence over feeling (as if the two can really be separated), and they're on the lookout for all the horrors that mothers supposedly inflict upon their children. They hold women far more responsible than men for every problem that troubles intimate relationships and family life, and expect women, rather than men, to make the changes that will help relationships function smoothly. They're fortified with a veritable arsenal (*The Diagnostic and Statistical Manual of Mental Disorders IV* is its current incarnation) of nasty labels for those, mostly women, who don't conform to traditional ideas of normalcy. Finally, having absorbed all these prejudices, and even as they inflict them on the people who seek their help, therapists somehow manage simultaneously to believe that they are "neutral," "impartial," and "objective." I use these three words because they are the jargon common to therapists.

I began to emerge from this kind of upside-down indoctrination, in which going along with so many biases is called "maintaining an attitude of neutrality," when I entered post-graduate training in family therapy at the Multicultural Family Institute in New Jersey. There and in later independent study, I read the work of thinkers who present a wider range of viewpoints. These include Paulo Freire; Riane Eisler, the sociologist and power theorist; John Stoltenberg, the pro-feminist theorist and activist; gay, lesbian, and transgender author/activists, including Audre Lorde, Urvashi Vaid, Suzanne Pharr, and Leslie Feinberg; and Native North American scholar/activists, such as Paula Gunn Allan and Vine Deloria, Jr. This reading—along with the guidance provided by the women and men of color, gay men and lesbians, and people with disabilities who were my teachers and peers—opened a window onto a reality I'd never encountered before. I owe an enormous debt of gratitude to these mentors.

I do not pretend to bring neutrality to my work. Instead, I help my clients uncover and challenge the powerful biases and imbalances in power that contribute to their problems. My political agenda may be more obvious than that of many therapists because mine seeks to replace domination with fairness and love, and that differs greatly from the mainstream political agenda of our time.

Q. Sometimes a person makes significant changes in their actions in order to improve their couple relationship, but their partner doesn't believe the changes will last. This can be very frustrating, making the person feel, "What's the point in changing?" What do you think about this?

A. Two of the PRINCIPLES OF LOVE from Chapter One are "Love needs constancy" and "It takes time for love to heal." When a person makes a positive change it takes time, sometimes a lot longer than feels comfortable, for their partner to believe the change will stick. That length of time depends upon a number of factors, including the impact of the negative behavior, how long it was going on, how much damage it created, and how much work it took to get a commitment for change.

To make matters even more frustrating, people often respond

irritably at first to their partner's positive change: "Why couldn't you have stayed within our budget two years ago like you were supposed to—I can't believe how much debt you still have to pay down!" This happens because a positive change brings relief, and with relief comes a flood of emotions that were pushed aside.

The person who changes their actions must avoid seeking validation from their partner because every, "See how much I've changed?" throws salt on the old wound. Instead, he or she should gather much-needed support from trusted friends. As the new pattern endures, it becomes more prominent than the history of pain, and, *eventually*, trustworthy for their partner.

Q. Are there good things about traditional male patterns of behavior?

A. Absolutely. The traditional value most men place upon courage, loyalty, and perseverance is a prime example. These are wonderful values when coupled with a vision of power that promotes love and collaboration.

Remember, the problem is not men, but rather a system of beliefs and behavior driven by the practice of power as domination. The problem is patriarchy. As members of couples, communities, institutions, and society, we face the challenge of solving the problem—breaking this dehumanizing system. The task stands large before us, but together we can create a better system—a reality formed from collaboration and the power of love. Each of us deserves nothing less.

Notes

✦ ✧ ✦

CHAPTER ONE: PRINCIPLES OF LOVE FOR THE 21ST CENTURY

1. "The principles of love are always the same . . .": bell hooks, *All About Love: New Visions* (New York: William Morrow and Co., 2000), 138.

2. bell hooks and Barbara Kingsolver: See bell hooks, *All About Love: New Visions* (New York: William Morrow and Co., 2000) for an extended discussion on the meaning of love and Barbara Kingsolver, *Small Wonder* (New York: Perennial, 2002), for reflections on love in the post 9/11/01 world.

CHAPTER TWO: THE NEW PROBLEM WITH NO NAME

14. another aspect of the "problem with no name": Betty Friedan, *The Feminine Mystique* (New York: Norton, 2001).

23. critical consciousness: Paulo Freire, *Education for Critical Consciousness* (New York: Continuum, 1973).

CHAPTER THREE: WHAT PATRIARCHY TEACHES MEN

29. violence prevention experts: Allan Creighton and Paul Kivel, *Helping Teens Stop Violence: A Practical Guide for Counselors, Educators, and Parents, with contributions from Harrison Simms, Carrie McCluer* (Alameda: Hunter House, 1990).

32. work of family therapy researcher: Robert Jay Green, Rhea Almeida, ed., "Traditional Norms of Masculinity," *Transformations of Gender and Race in Family Therapy* (Binghamton: Haworth Press, 1998), 81–83.

39. In *From Brotherhood to Manhood:* Anderson J. Franklin, *From Brotherhood to Manhood: How Black Men Rescue Their Relationships and Dreams from the Invisibility Syndrome* (Hoboken: John Wiley & Sons, Inc., 2004), 105.

46. They found it unacceptable: Alice Walker, *The Same River Twice: Honoring the Difficult* (New York: Washington Square Press, 1996), for her story of the movie's making and what followed.

CHAPTER FOUR: IS MY PARTNER LISTENING IMPAIRED?

55. The title of Laura Schlessinger's book, *The Proper Care and Feeding of Husbands:* Laura Schlessinger, *The Proper Care and Feeding of Husbands* (New York: HarperCollins, 2004).

56. "Nope . . . what women accept . . . ": *An Interview with Dr. Laura Schlessinger* (HarperCollins.com, 2003).

61. Psychologist John Gray has made a fortune: John Gray, *Men Are From Mars, Women Are From Venus: A Practical Guide for Improving Communication and Getting What You Want in Your Relationships* (New York: HarperCollins, 1992).

CHAPTER FIVE: A CLOSER LOOK AT POWER

73. Drawn from personal experiences described by entertainers Danny Glover and Harry Belafonte: Bobbie Battista. (Host). *Talk Back Live: Is There Racial Discrimination in New York Cabs?* [Television broadcast] (Atlanta: Cable News Network, November 12, 1999, 3:00PM, ET).

77. . . . whenever I decide to "out" myself as a gay man: If you were enjoying the book up to this point but have decided to read no further, that's homophobia. Homophobia is an attitude of fear or hatred toward gay people. I'm assuming that few readers experienced this reaction because those prone to doing so would likely have abandoned the book much earlier on, at the first mention of gay and transgender people.

90. For a deeper look at the two: Riane Eisler, *The Chalice and the Blade* (San Francisco: HarperCollins, 1987).

CHAPTER SIX: RECOGNIZING ABUSE

113. I asked Miriam to look: See Appendix A

122. Researchers Edward Gondolf and David Russell: Edward Gondolf and David Russell, "The Case Against Anger Control Treatment Programs for Batterers," *Response,* vol. 9 #3, 1986, 2-5.

CHAPTER SEVEN: BEWARE THERAPISTS AND OTHER "HELPERS"

135. ". . . different behaviors to spice things up . . . ": William O'Hanlon-Hudson and Patricia Hudson-O'Hanlon, *Love is a Verb: How to Stop Analyzing your Relationship and Start Making it Great!* (New York: Norton, 1995), 49.

137. ". . . give love in a way that he or she recognized . . . ": Ibid., 37.

139. Michael Nichols, in *The Lost Art of Listening:* Michael Nichols, *The Lost Art of Listening* (New York: Guilford Press, 1995).

139. ". . . he has to drive them somewhere.": Ibid., 143.

141. ". . . deep and ugly fears of worthlessness . . . ": Ibid., 90.

142. "That is part of the violence." David R. Grove and Jay Haley, *Conversations on Therapy* (New York: Norton, 1993), 77.

142. ". . . and rejection—until he explodes." Harville Hendrix, *Keeping the Love You Find: A Guide for Singles* (New York: Pocket Books, 1992), 125.

143. ". . . like fairness and inequality and so on." Michael Nichols, *The Lost Art of Listening* (New York: Guilford Press, 1995), 205.

143. " . . . burdened with a sense of imperfect masculinity." Frank Pittman, *Man Enough: Fathers, Sons, and the Search for Masculinity* (New York: Putnam, 1993), 33.

144. ". . . too busy to stir up much trouble." Ibid., 242.

144. ". . . money and better care of him." Ibid., 240.

144. ". . . unpleasant topic had been brought up." Ibid., 30.

CHAPTER EIGHT: TRANSFORMING THE MALE CODE

153. family therapy colleagues Roberto Font and Rhea Almeida: Kenneth Dolan-Del Vecchio, Roberto Font, and Rhea Almeida, ed., "Expanded Norms of The Male Role," *Transformations of Gender and Race in Family Therapy* (Binghamton: Haworth Press, 1998), 96–97.

166. any such international judicial matter: Rahul Mahajan, *Full Spectrum Dominance: US Power in Iraq and Beyond* (New York: Seven Stories Press, 2003), 33–35. Noam Chomsky, *Hegemony or Survival: America's Quest for Global Dominance* (New York: Metropolitan Books, 2003), 199.

171. interviewed then-Secretary of State Madeleine Albright: Lesley Stahl, "Punishing Saddam," produced by Catherine Olian, CBS, *60 Minutes,* May 12, 1996.

CHAPTER NINE: MEN CAN BE HEROES!

186. Nathan McCall's books: *Makes Me Wanna Holler: A Young Black Man in America* (New York: Vintage Books, 1995); *What's Going On: Personal Essays* (New York: Random House, 1997).

186. *Men's Work: How to Stop the Violence That Tears Our Lives Apart:* Paul Kivel, (New York: Ballantine Books, 1992).

186. John Stoltenberg's *Refusing to be a Man:*(New York: Meridian, 1989).

186. Leslie Feinberg's *Trans Liberation: Beyond Pink or Blue:* (Boston: Beacon Press, 1996).

CHAPTER TEN: CREATING LASTING CHANGE

214. Or, as bell hooks writes: bell hooks, *All About Love: New Visions* (William Morrow and Company: New York, 2000), 19.

Chapter Eleven: Dialogue

221. In their book, *Warrior Marks*: Alice Walker and Pratibha Parmar, *Warrior Marks: genital mutilation and the sexual blinding of women* (New York: Harvest Books, 1993).

222. A number of excellent books: Claudia Bepko and JoAnn Krestan, *Too Good for Her Own Good: Breaking Free From the Burden of Female Responsibility* (New York: Harper & Row, 1990); Susan Maushart, *Wifework: What Marriage Really Means for Women* (New York: Bloomsbury, 2001); Harriet Lerner, *The Dance of Anger: A Woman's Guide to Changing the Patterns of Intimate Relationships* (New York: Harper & Row, 1985); Harriet Lerner, *The Dance of Intimacy: A Woman's Guide to Courageous Acts of Change in Key Relationships* (New York: Harper & Row, 1989).

223. Introduced by Brazilian educator Paulo Freire: Paulo Freire, *Education for Critical Consciousness* (New York: Continuum, 1973).

Appendix: Power and Control Wheel

✦ ◇ ✦

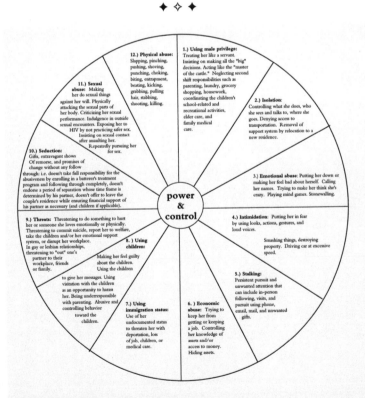

Adapted from Ellen Pence & Michael Paymar. *Educational Groups For Men Who Batter: The Duluth Model.* (New York: Springer Publishing, 1993).

Acknowledgments

✦ ✧ ✦

First, I thank the men, women, and families who over the years have trusted me enough to seek my counsel. They teach me volumes about love, courage, and justice.

Joy E. Stocke helped me craft a thorough book proposal. With charm, good humor, and unflagging encouragement, she taught me the rewards of perseverance, and something of the business of writing. I am forever in her debt.

I thank Judith Lockard for reading an early draft of the manuscript, for sharing helpful advice, and for introducing me to Joy Stocke.

I thank Judith Levy for the life coaching. She must know what she's doing as my goal of completing this book has been achieved.

Friends and colleagues read various versions of the manuscript and lent invaluable criticism. These include Lucille Grey, Shirley Cresci, Heidi Remak, and Bill Rotchford. I give special thanks to those who wrote endorsements before I even had a publisher, including Michael Kimmel, Pilar Hernandez, Rhea Almeida, and Alan Youngblood.

I thank Monica McGoldrick, Nydia Garcia Preto, Roberto Font, Theresa Messineo, and Rosemary Woods for empowering me to see white male supremacy and challenge it in myself and in the world. I thank them also for introducing me to family systems theory.

My friend and colleague Garry Giannone helped in a multitude of ways. I have endless gratitude for his presence in my life.

Lynn Parker and I barely survived a wild journey writing a family therapy textbook together at the same time as I wrote this book. I cherish her like a war buddy. Lynn wrote an endorsement, critiqued the manuscript, and pointed out that one of the early covers resembled soft porn. She's smart, funny, and fierce. Semper Fi, Lynn.

Jo-Lynne Worley gave helpful recommendations. She linked me to Stephanie von Hirschberg, who provided thoughtful advice on the book proposal.

Nocona Pewewardy and Tim Wise, warriors for justice, are links in my chain of good fortune. Nocona brought my work to Tim's attention, and he pointed me toward Richard Nash.

Richard Nash, my publisher, stands alone. At every stage of development his kindness and clarity enriched this work. Richard, and the rest of the team at Soft Skull—as my son would say—you rock!

I thank David Drummond and Sterling McAndrew, a couple whose friendship means the world to me. (David repeatedly insisted that he be mentioned. I hope this quiets him.)

Sue Meadows threw me a surprise book party long before I had a contract. A better friend I'll never find. Sue tells the truth even when it's going to hurt. Now that's love!

I thank Cyndie Fearon for her tireless work to end domestic violence, for her endless encouragement, and for always finding a reason to laugh. I love her like the sister I never had. And I thank her for my new Easter greeting: "She is risen indeed!"

Terry Ginder and Gretchen Walsh hired me into the strange world of corporations. What I expected would be a brief respite from the insanity of managed mental health care somehow became a way of life. I love them just the same.

Pasquale Del Vecchio, my paternal grandfather and an elderly man by the time I came along, raised hell during his youth. He challenged his elders in Gallo, the Neapolitan mountain village of his birth, to question their priests instead of following blindly. After emigrating from Italy to the U.S., he refused to join the bloodbath of World War I and landed in jail as a result. I thank him for his legacy of courageous resistance.

Isabel Nelson Dill, my maternal grandmother, loved me greatly when I was a little boy. The warmth that I feel when remembering her reminds me of the power that love brings. I will always be grateful to her.

I thank Lynn Dolan, the mother of my son. Wise, fearless, and loving—she is the best co-parent one could hope for. During the writing of this book our son, Erik Dolan-Del Vecchio, grew into a renaissance teenager. He plays electric guitar and bass in a rock band and violin in his school's orchestra, shows a growing passion for the study of history, and observes human and institutional behavior with clarity beyond his years. He inspires me to believe that in his generation the madness of patriarchy may finally meet its match.

My parents, Joseph and Barbara Del Vecchio, taught me by their example to value people, fairness, and learning more than money. Quiet revolutionaries, I hope to honor them by turning up the volume a notch or two.

Finally, I thank my partner, Tim Garrett. A brilliant writer, powerful in all the best ways, and endlessly loving, Tim sharpened the manuscript immeasurably with his comments. I thank him for being the source of much that is good in my life.